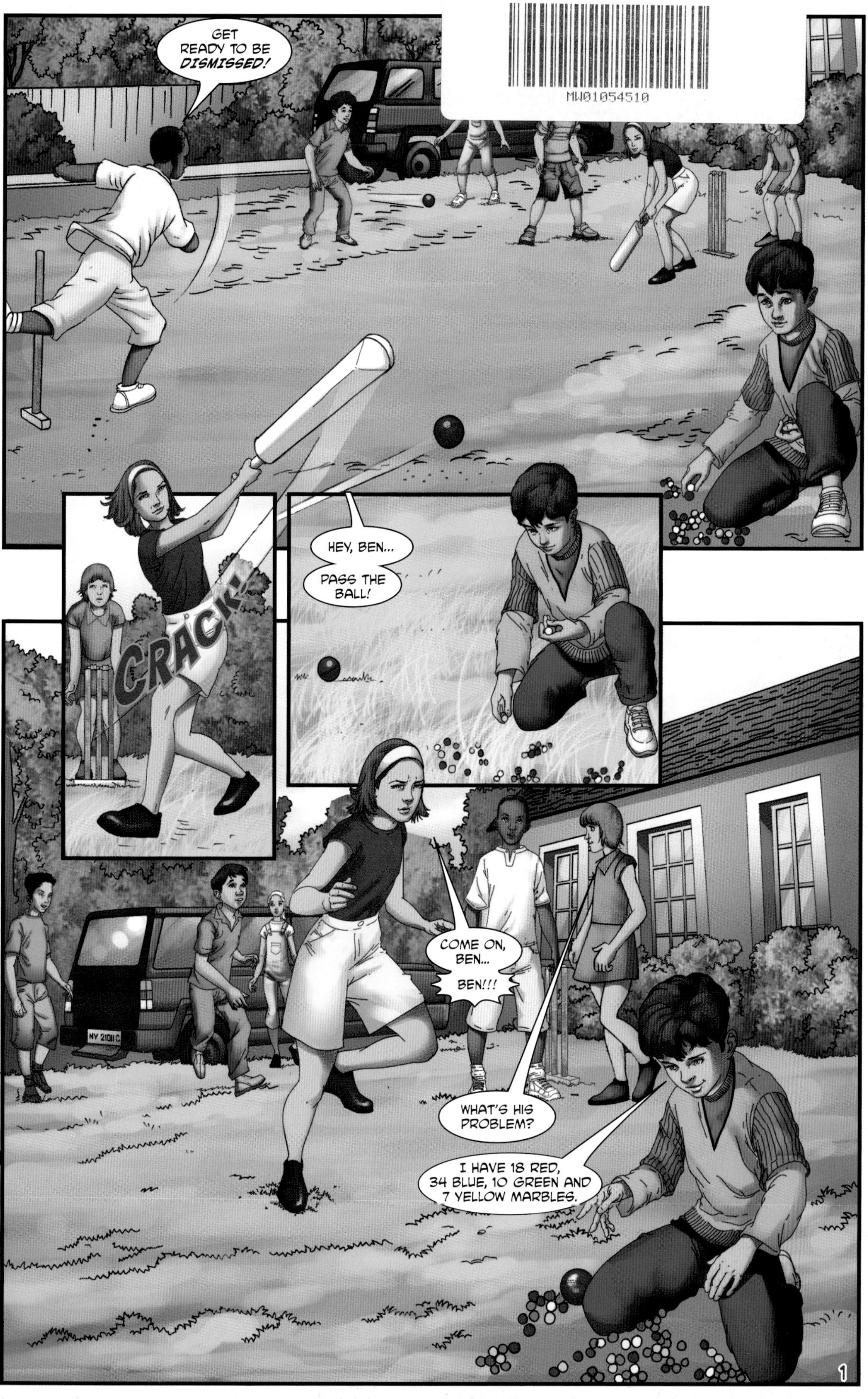
GET READY TO BE DISMISSED!
CRACK!
HEY, BEN...
PASS THE BALL!
COME ON, BEN...
BEN!!!
WHAT'S HIS PROBLEM?
I HAVE 18 RED, 34 BLUE, 10 GREEN AND 7 YELLOW MARBLES.

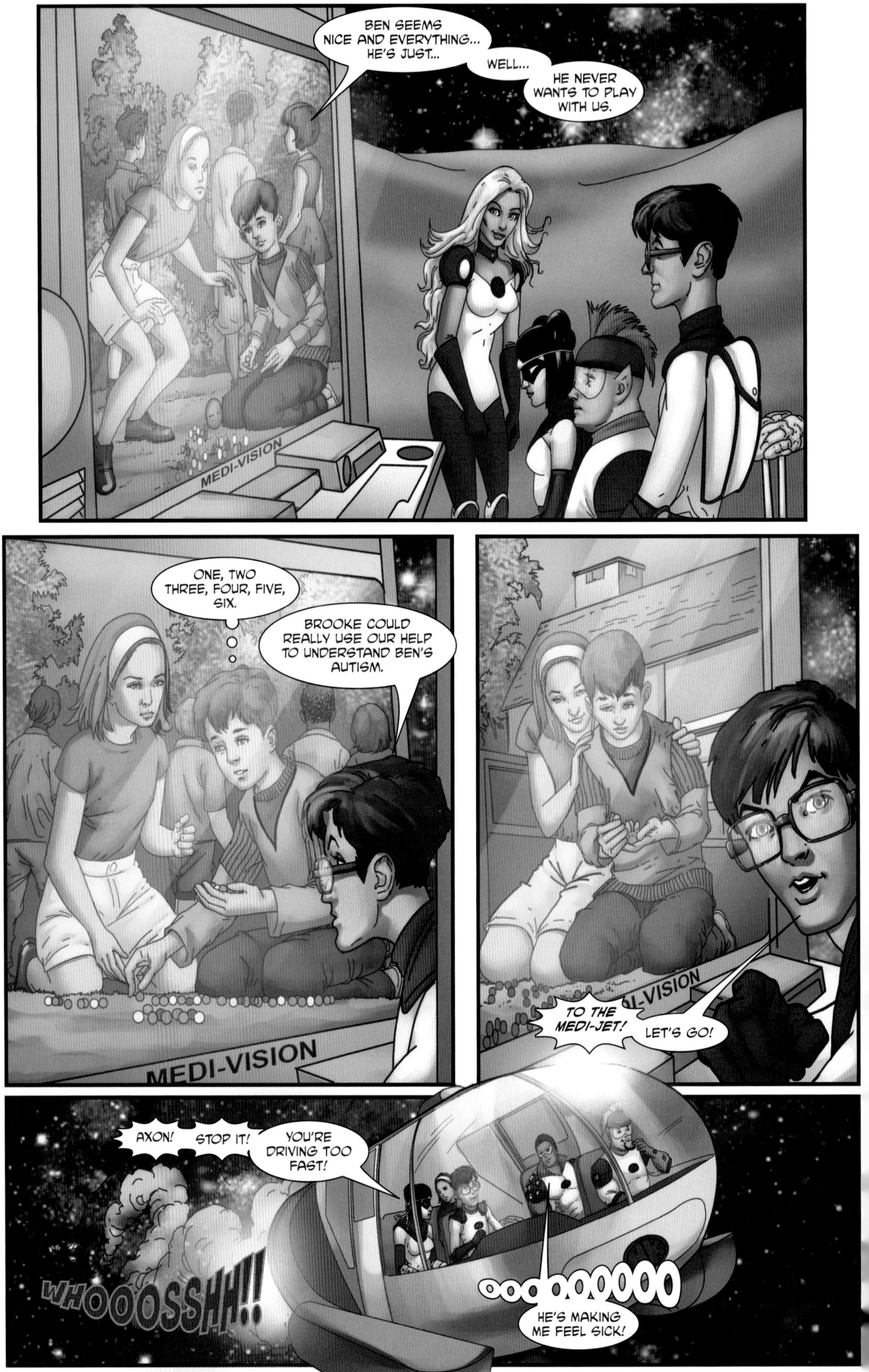
BEN SEEMS NICE AND EVERYTHING... HE'S JUST...
WELL...
HE NEVER WANTS TO PLAY WITH US.
MEDI-VISION
ONE, TWO THREE, FOUR, FIVE, SIX.
BROOKE COULD REALLY USE OUR HELP TO UNDERSTAND BEN'S AUTISM.
MEDI-VISION
...I-VISION
TO THE MEDI-JET!
LET'S GO!
AXON!
STOP IT!
YOU'RE DRIVING TOO FAST!
WHOOOOSSHH!!
OOOOOOOOO
HE'S MAKING ME FEEL SICK!

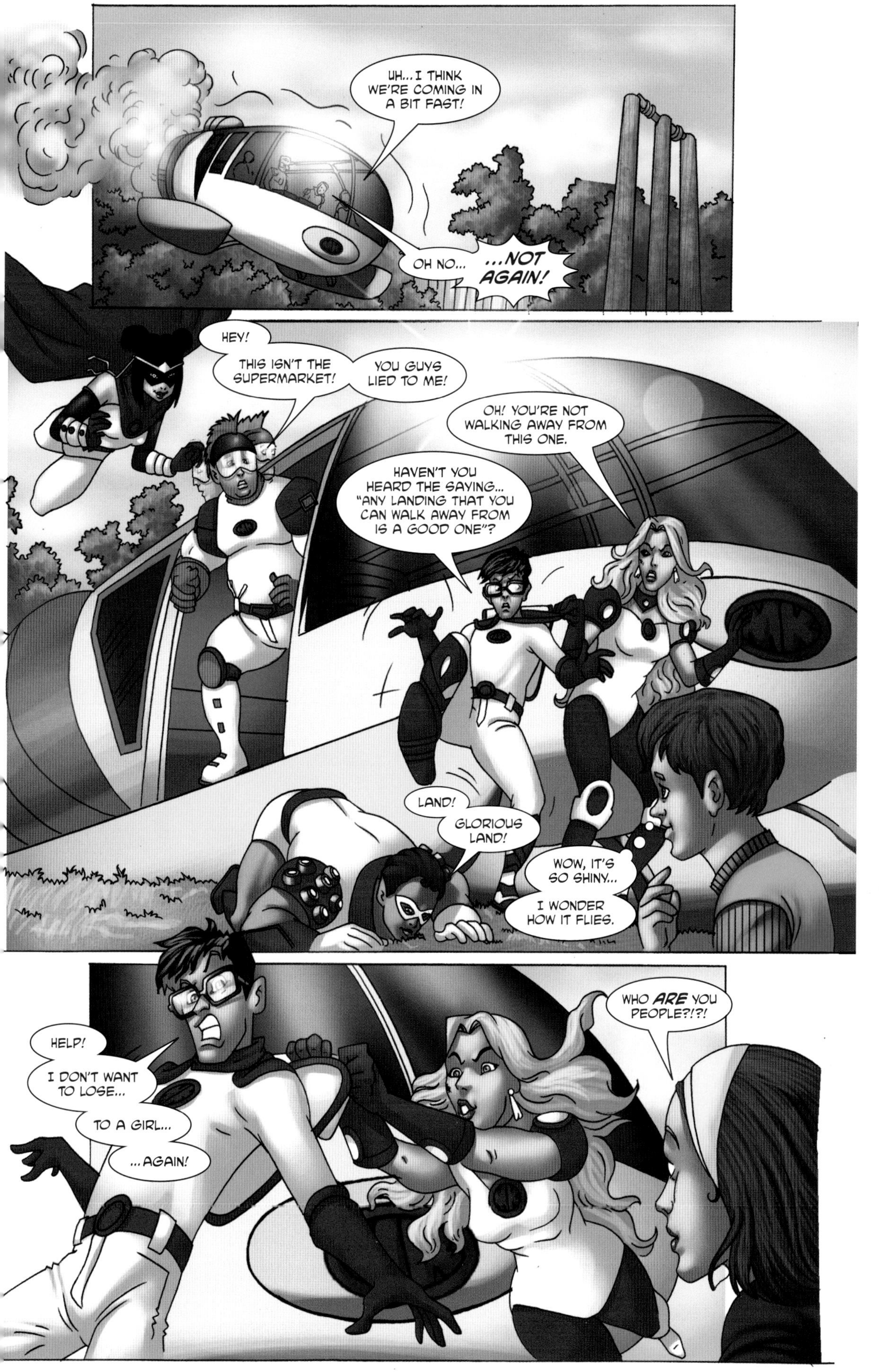
UH... I THINK WE'RE COMING IN A BIT FAST!
OH NO...
...NOT AGAIN!
HEY!
THIS ISN'T THE SUPERMARKET!
YOU GUYS LIED TO ME!
OH! YOU'RE NOT WALKING AWAY FROM THIS ONE.
HAVEN'T YOU HEARD THE SAYING... "ANY LANDING THAT YOU CAN WALK AWAY FROM IS A GOOD ONE"?
LAND!
GLORIOUS LAND!
WOW, IT'S SO SHINY...
I WONDER HOW IT FLIES.
HELP!
I DON'T WANT TO LOSE...
TO A GIRL...
...AGAIN!
WHO ARE YOU PEOPLE?!?!

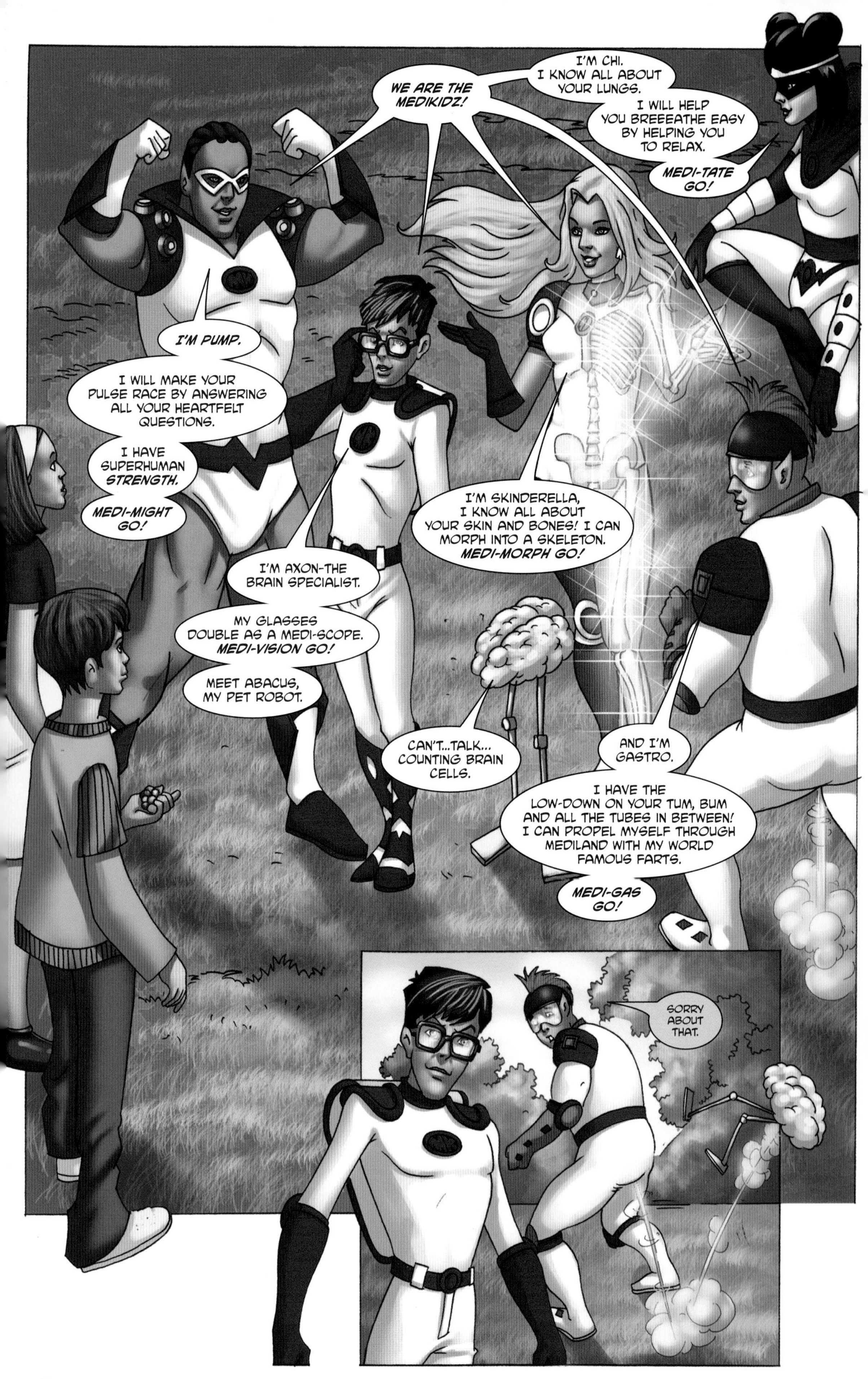
WE ARE THE MEDIKIDZ!
I'M CHI. I KNOW ALL ABOUT YOUR LUNGS.
I WILL HELP YOU BREEEATHE EASY BY HELPING YOU TO RELAX.
MEDI-TATE GO!
I'M PUMP.
I WILL MAKE YOUR PULSE RACE BY ANSWERING ALL YOUR HEARTFELT QUESTIONS.
I HAVE SUPERHUMAN STRENGTH.
MEDI-MIGHT GO!
I'M SKINDERELLA, I KNOW ALL ABOUT YOUR SKIN AND BONES! I CAN MORPH INTO A SKELETON. MEDI-MORPH GO!
I'M AXON-THE BRAIN SPECIALIST.
MY GLASSES DOUBLE AS A MEDI-SCOPE. MEDI-VISION GO!
MEET ABACUS, MY PET ROBOT.
CAN'T...TALK... COUNTING BRAIN CELLS.
AND I'M GASTRO.
I HAVE THE LOW-DOWN ON YOUR TUM, BUM AND ALL THE TUBES IN BETWEEN! I CAN PROPEL MYSELF THROUGH MEDILAND WITH MY WORLD FAMOUS FARTS.
MEDI-GAS GO!
SORRY ABOUT THAT.

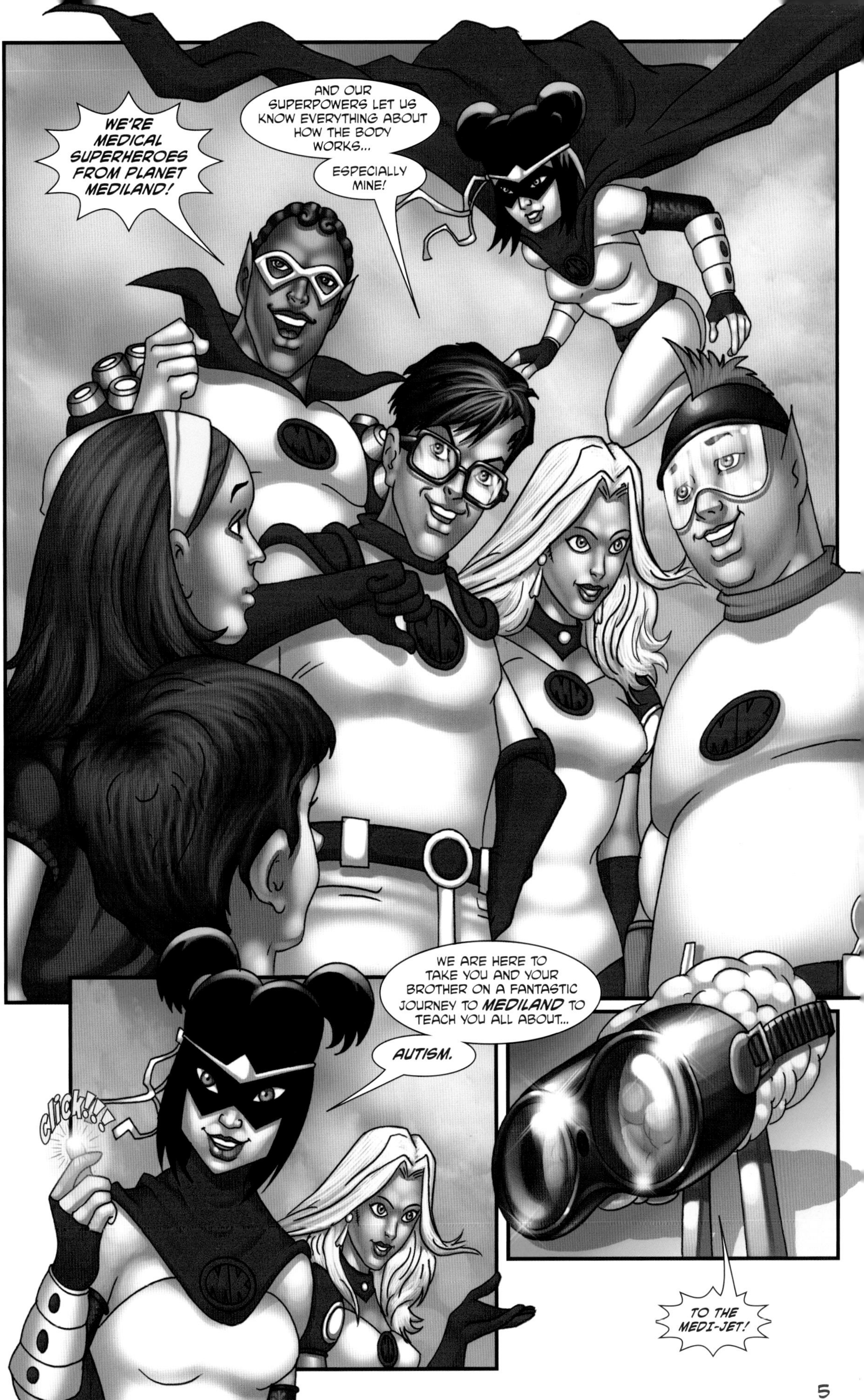
WE'RE MEDICAL SUPERHEROES FROM PLANET MEDILAND!
AND OUR SUPERPOWERS LET US KNOW EVERYTHING ABOUT HOW THE BODY WORKS...
ESPECIALLY MINE!
WE ARE HERE TO TAKE YOU AND YOUR BROTHER ON A FANTASTIC JOURNEY TO MEDILAND TO TEACH YOU ALL ABOUT...
AUTISM.
click!!!
TO THE MEDI-JET!

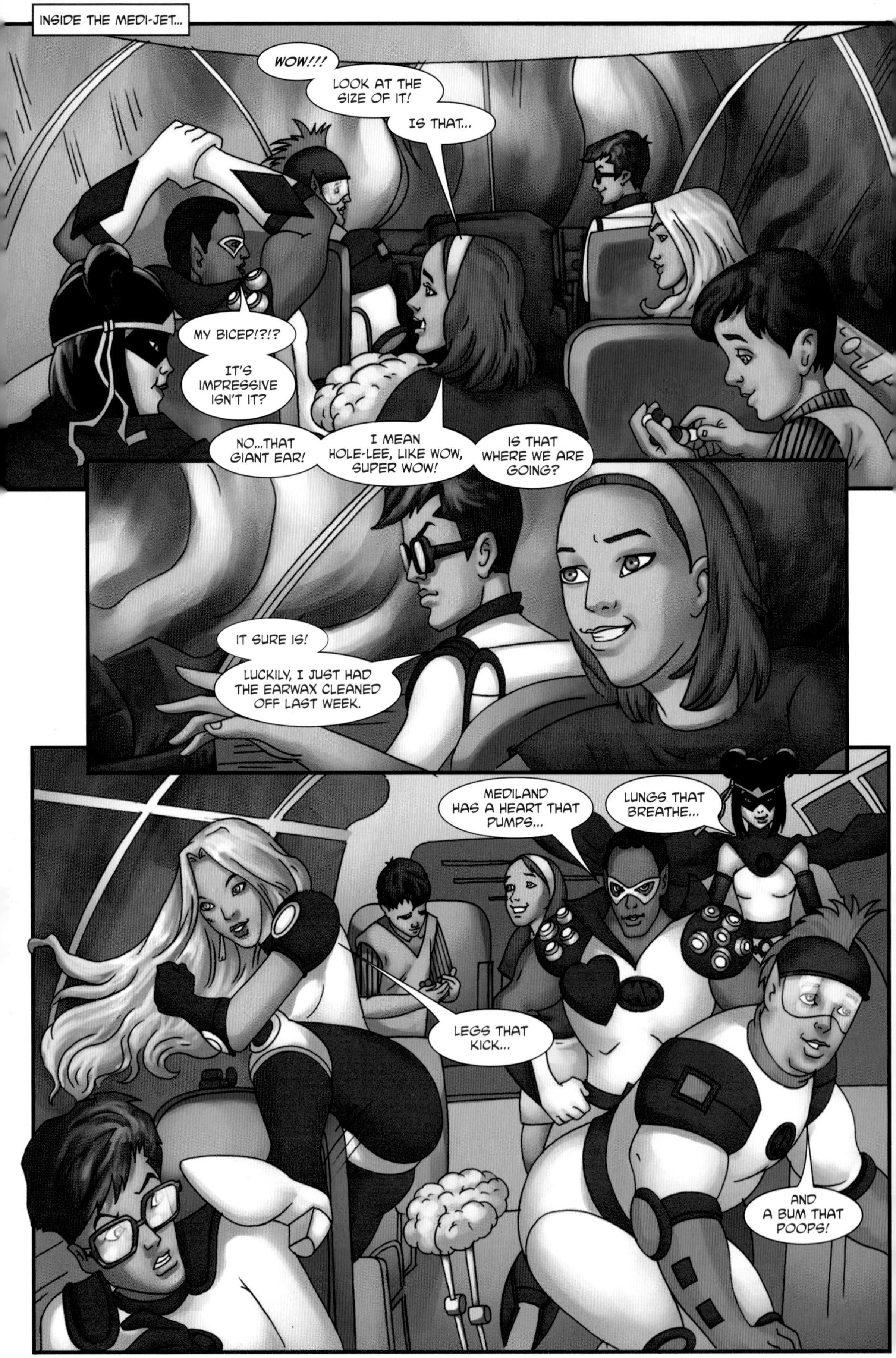

INSIDE THE MEDI-JET...
WOW!!!
LOOK AT THE SIZE OF IT!
IS THAT...
MY BICEP!?!?
IT'S IMPRESSIVE ISN'T IT?
NO...THAT GIANT EAR!
I MEAN HOLE-LEE, LIKE WOW, SUPER WOW!
IS THAT WHERE WE ARE GOING?
IT SURE IS!
LUCKILY, I JUST HAD THE EARWAX CLEANED OFF LAST WEEK.
MEDILAND HAS A HEART THAT PUMPS...
LUNGS THAT BREATHE...
LEGS THAT KICK...
AND A BUM THAT POOPS!

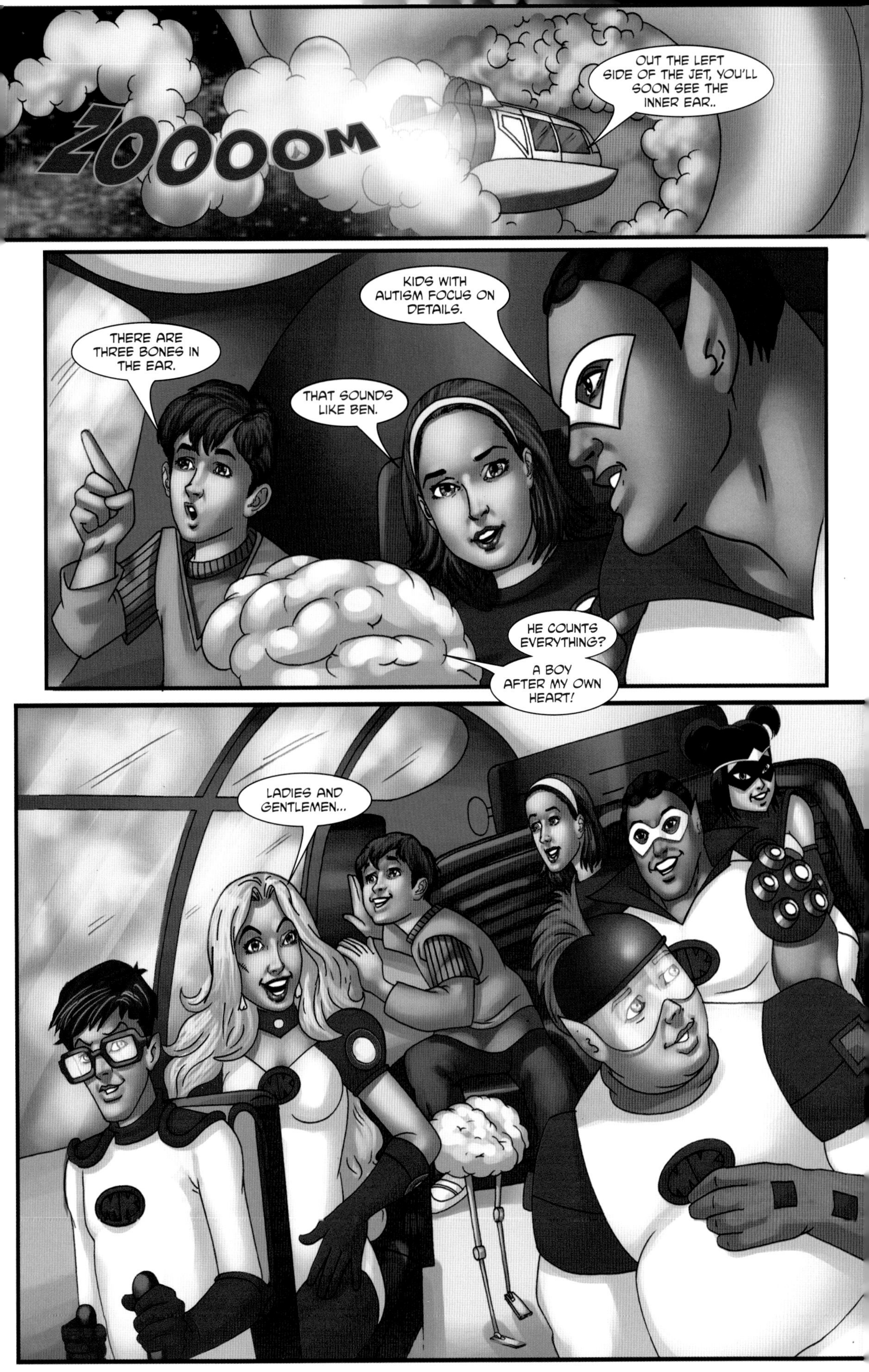
ZOOOOM
OUT THE LEFT SIDE OF THE JET, YOU'LL SOON SEE THE INNER EAR..
THERE ARE THREE BONES IN THE EAR.
KIDS WITH AUTISM FOCUS ON DETAILS.
THAT SOUNDS LIKE BEN.
HE COUNTS EVERYTHING?
A BOY AFTER MY OWN HEART!
LADIES AND GENTLEMEN...

...WELCOME TO THE BRAIN!

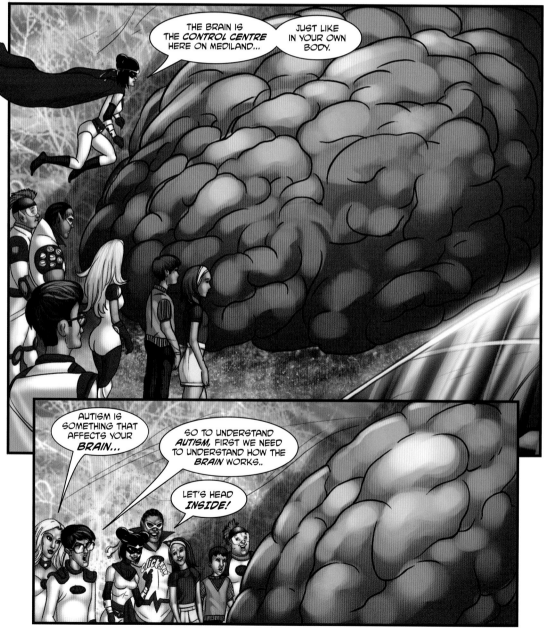

THE BRAIN IS THE *CONTROL CENTRE* HERE ON MEDILAND...

JUST LIKE IN YOUR OWN BODY.

AUTISM IS SOMETHING THAT AFFECTS YOUR *BRAIN*...

SO TO UNDERSTAND *AUTISM,* FIRST WE NEED TO UNDERSTAND HOW THE *BRAIN* WORKS..

LET'S HEAD *INSIDE!*

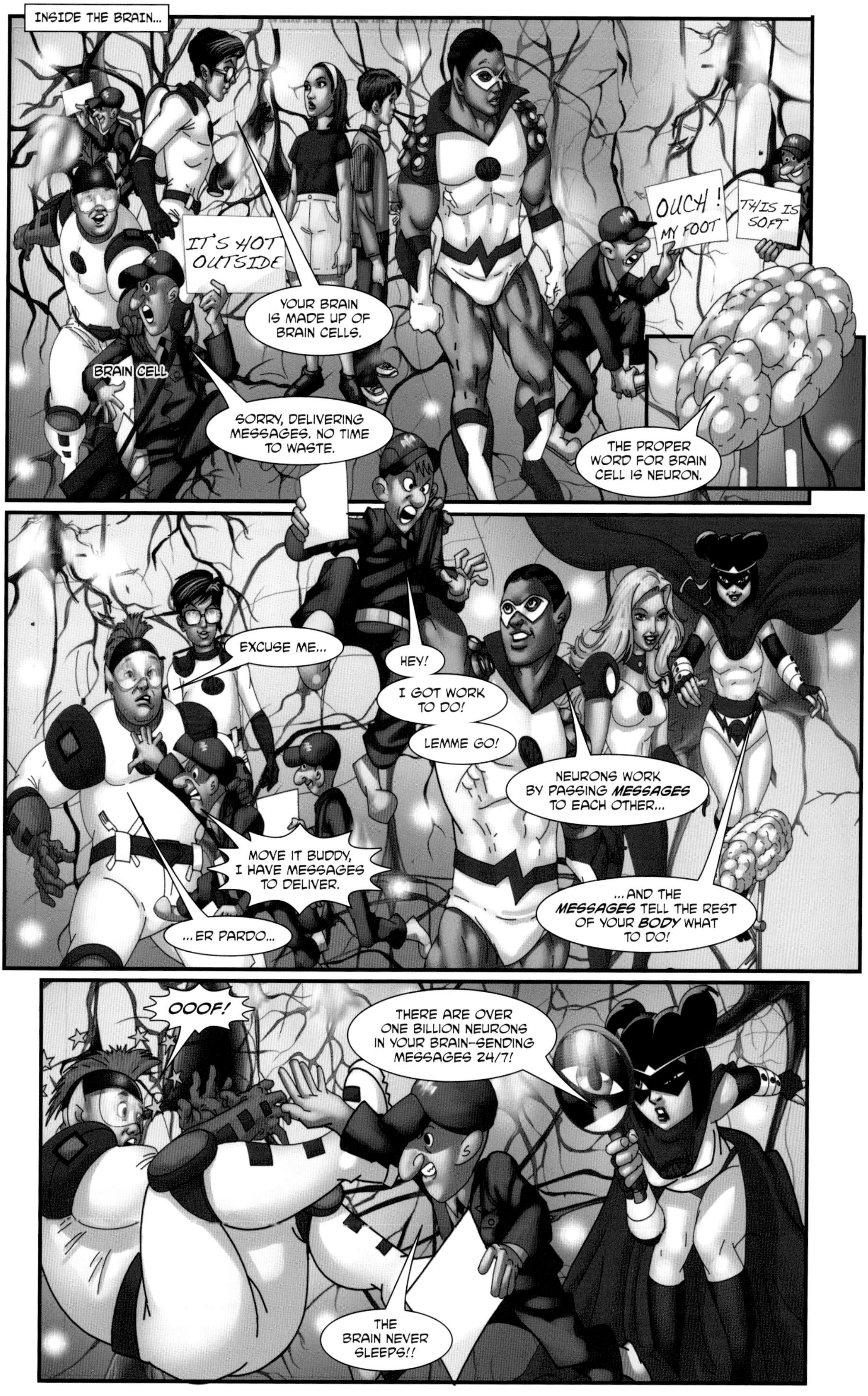
INSIDE THE BRAIN...
IT'S HOT OUTSIDE
YOUR BRAIN IS MADE UP OF BRAIN CELLS.
BRAIN CELL
SORRY, DELIVERING MESSAGES. NO TIME TO WASTE.
OUCH! MY FOOT
THIS IS SOFT
THE PROPER WORD FOR BRAIN CELL IS NEURON.
EXCUSE ME...
HEY!
I GOT WORK TO DO!
LEMME GO!
NEURONS WORK BY PASSING MESSAGES TO EACH OTHER...
MOVE IT BUDDY, I HAVE MESSAGES TO DELIVER.
...ER PARDO...
...AND THE MESSAGES TELL THE REST OF YOUR BODY WHAT TO DO!
OOOF!
THERE ARE OVER ONE BILLION NEURONS IN YOUR BRAIN–SENDING MESSAGES 24/7!
THE BRAIN NEVER SLEEPS!!

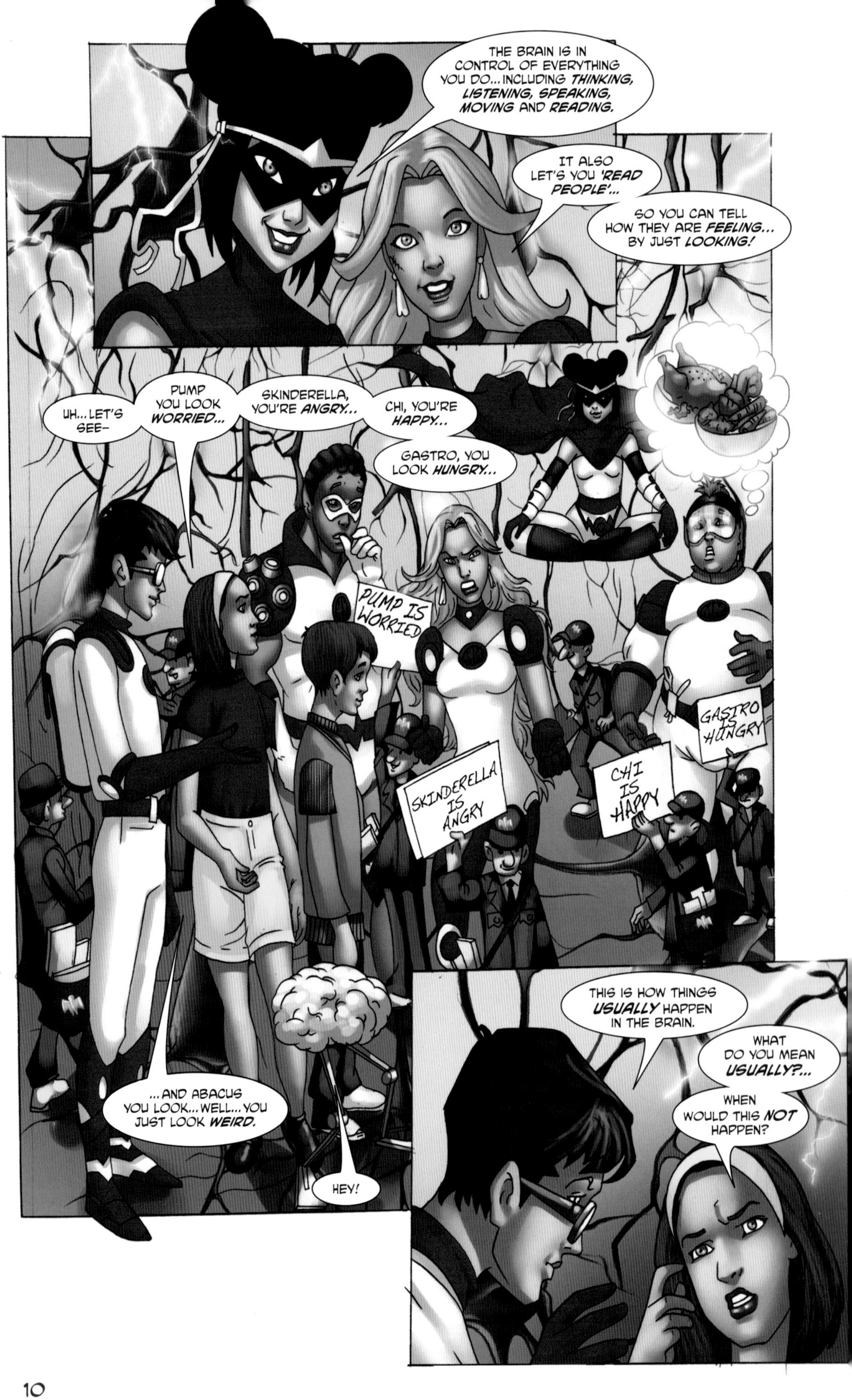
THE BRAIN IS IN CONTROL OF EVERYTHING YOU DO... INCLUDING THINKING, LISTENING, SPEAKING, MOVING AND READING.
IT ALSO LET'S YOU 'READ PEOPLE'...
SO YOU CAN TELL HOW THEY ARE FEELING... BY JUST LOOKING!
UH... LET'S SEE-
PUMP YOU LOOK WORRIED...
SKINDERELLA, YOU'RE ANGRY...
CHI, YOU'RE HAPPY...
GASTRO, YOU LOOK HUNGRY...
PUMP IS WORRIED
SKINDERELLA IS ANGRY
CHI IS HAPPY
GASTRO IS HUNGRY
...AND ABACUS YOU LOOK... WELL... YOU JUST LOOK WEIRD.
HEY!
THIS IS HOW THINGS USUALLY HAPPEN IN THE BRAIN.
WHAT DO YOU MEAN USUALLY?...
WHEN WOULD THIS NOT HAPPEN?

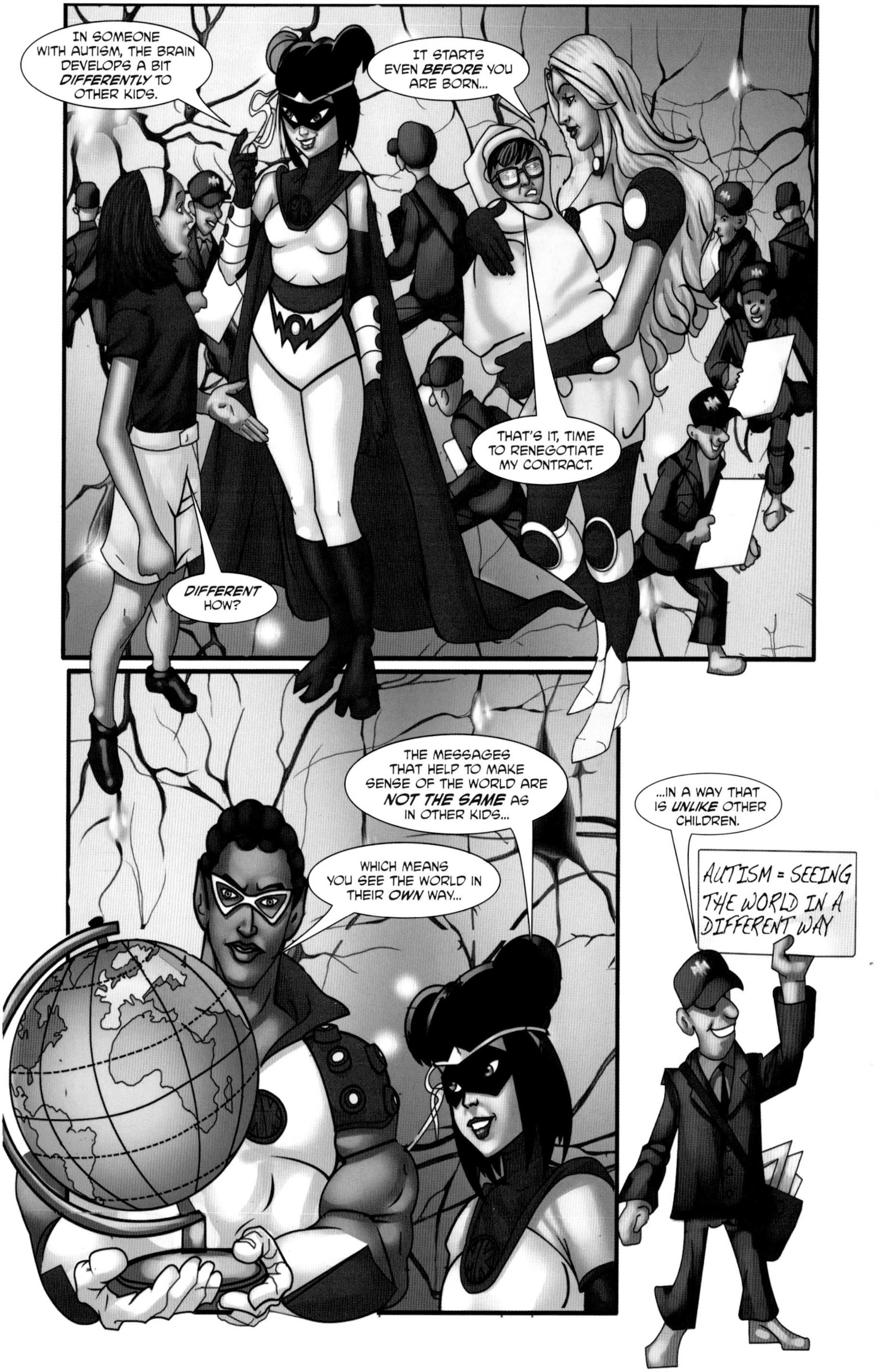
IN SOMEONE WITH AUTISM, THE BRAIN DEVELOPS A BIT DIFFERENTLY TO OTHER KIDS.
DIFFERENT HOW?
IT STARTS EVEN BEFORE YOU ARE BORN...
THAT'S IT, TIME TO RENEGOTIATE MY CONTRACT.
THE MESSAGES THAT HELP TO MAKE SENSE OF THE WORLD ARE NOT THE SAME AS IN OTHER KIDS...
WHICH MEANS YOU SEE THE WORLD IN THEIR OWN WAY...
...IN A WAY THAT IS UNLIKE OTHER CHILDREN.
AUTISM = SEEING THE WORLD IN A DIFFERENT WAY

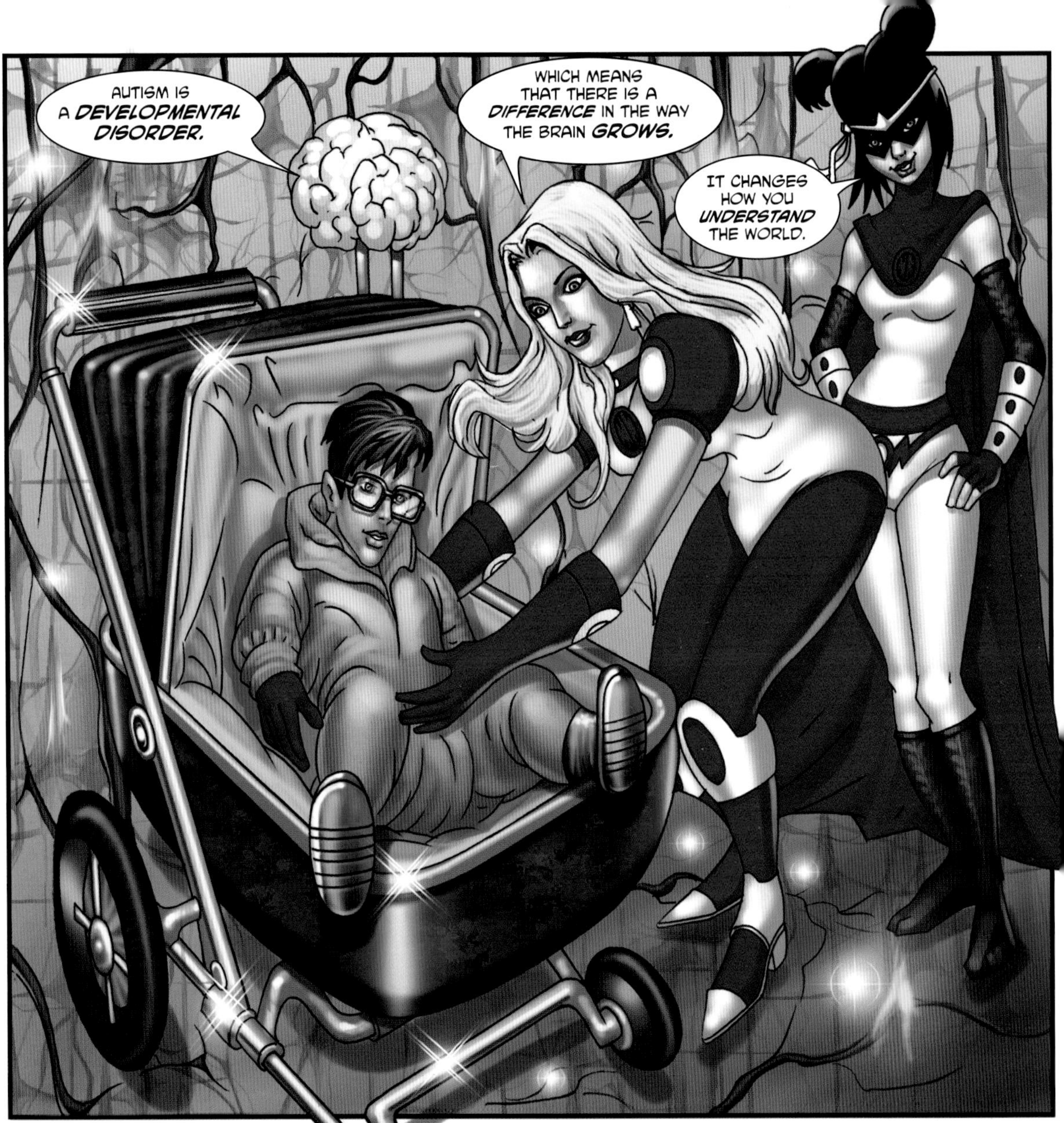
AUTISM IS A DEVELOPMENTAL DISORDER.
WHICH MEANS THAT THERE IS A DIFFERENCE IN THE WAY THE BRAIN GROWS.
IT CHANGES HOW YOU UNDERSTAND THE WORLD.

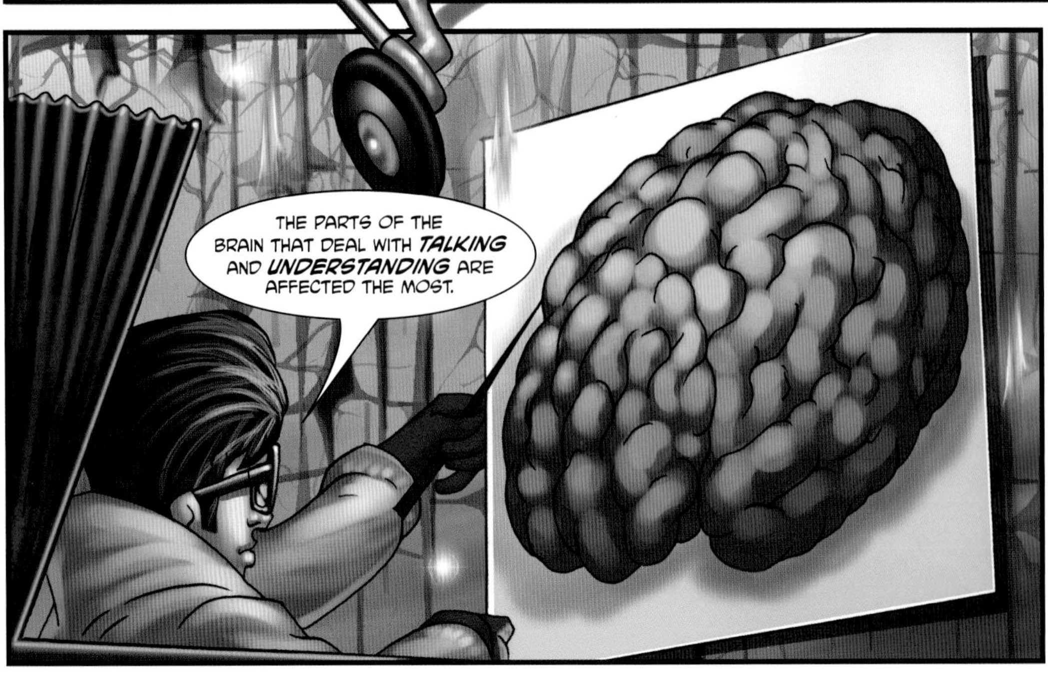
THE PARTS OF THE BRAIN THAT DEAL WITH TALKING AND UNDERSTANDING ARE AFFECTED THE MOST.

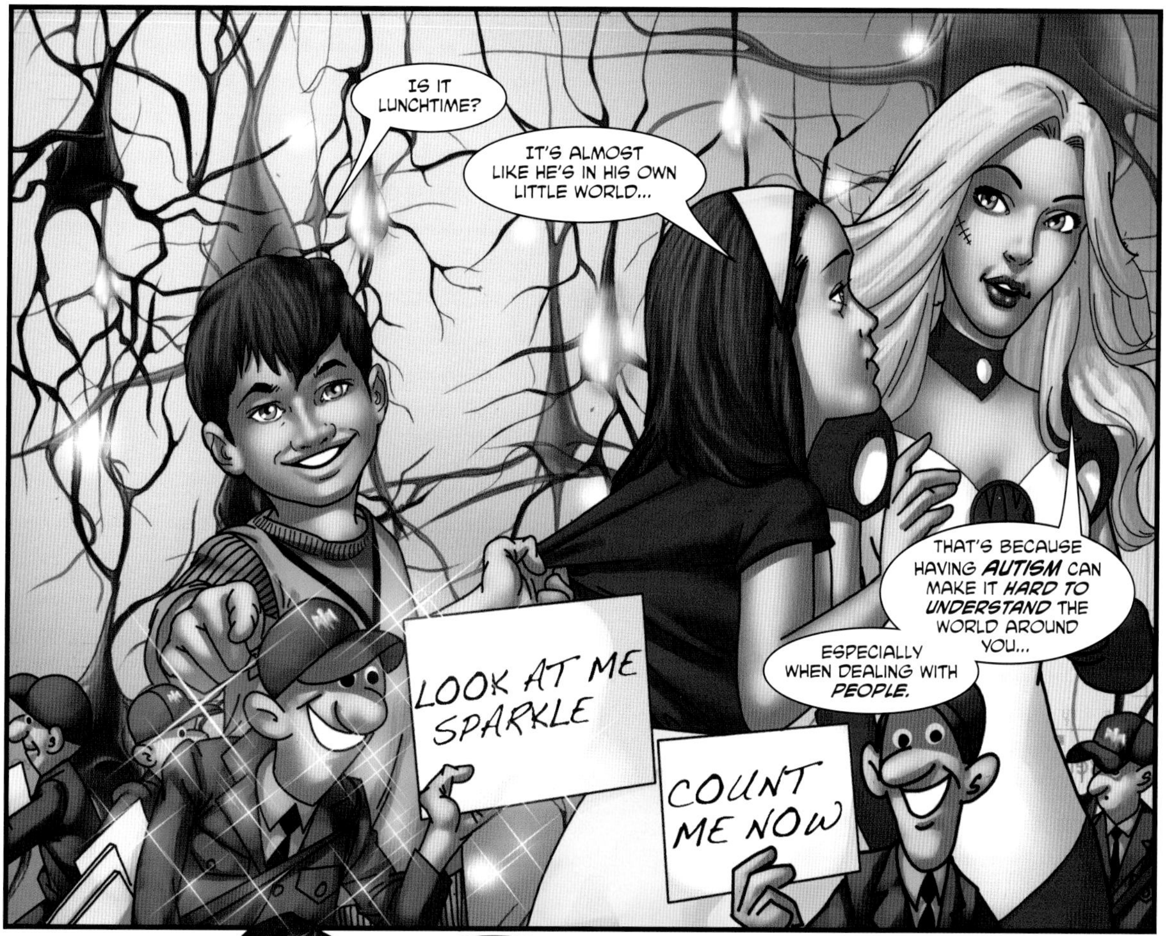
IS IT LUNCHTIME?
IT'S ALMOST LIKE HE'S IN HIS OWN LITTLE WORLD...
THAT'S BECAUSE HAVING **AUTISM** CAN MAKE IT **HARD TO UNDERSTAND** THE WORLD AROUND YOU...
ESPECIALLY WHEN DEALING WITH **PEOPLE.**
LOOK AT ME SPARKLE
COUNT ME NOW

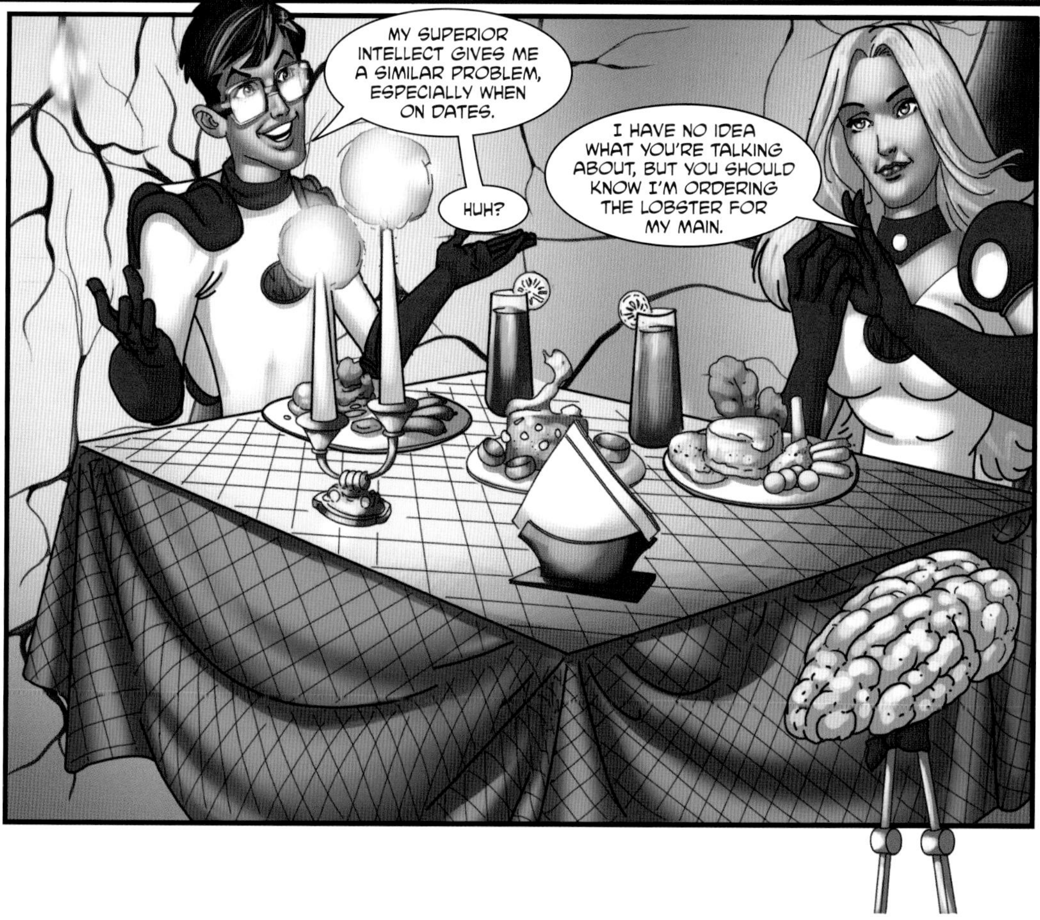
MY SUPERIOR INTELLECT GIVES ME A SIMILAR PROBLEM, ESPECIALLY WHEN ON DATES.
HUH?
I HAVE NO IDEA WHAT YOU'RE TALKING ABOUT, BUT YOU SHOULD KNOW I'M ORDERING THE LOBSTER FOR MY MAIN.

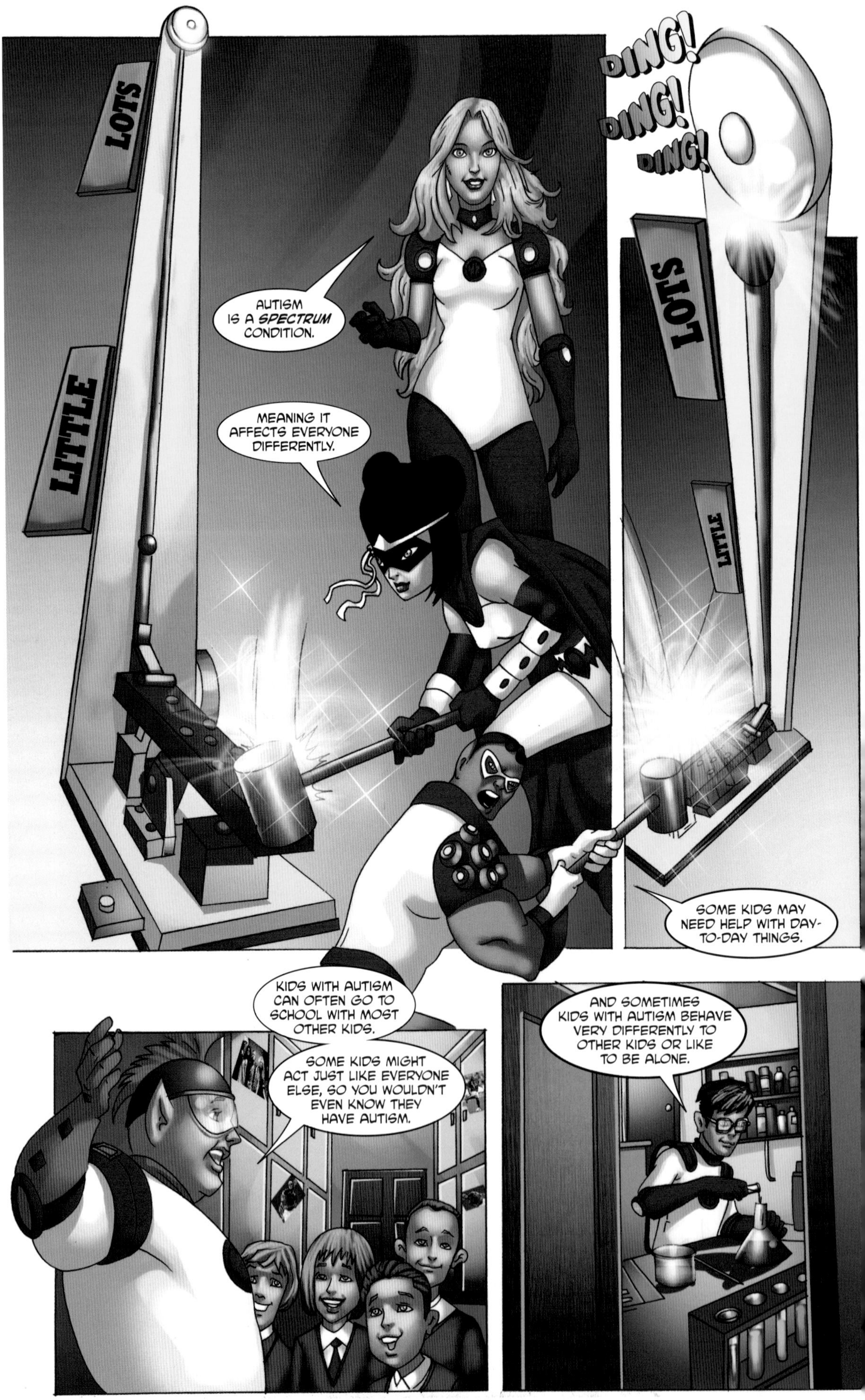
LOTS
LITTLE
AUTISM IS A *SPECTRUM* CONDITION.
MEANING IT AFFECTS EVERYONE DIFFERENTLY.
DING! DING! DING!
LOTS
LITTLE
SOME KIDS MAY NEED HELP WITH DAY-TO-DAY THINGS.
KIDS WITH AUTISM CAN OFTEN GO TO SCHOOL WITH MOST OTHER KIDS.
SOME KIDS MIGHT ACT JUST LIKE EVERYONE ELSE, SO YOU WOULDN'T EVEN KNOW THEY HAVE AUTISM.
AND SOMETIMES KIDS WITH AUTISM BEHAVE VERY DIFFERENTLY TO OTHER KIDS OR LIKE TO BE ALONE.

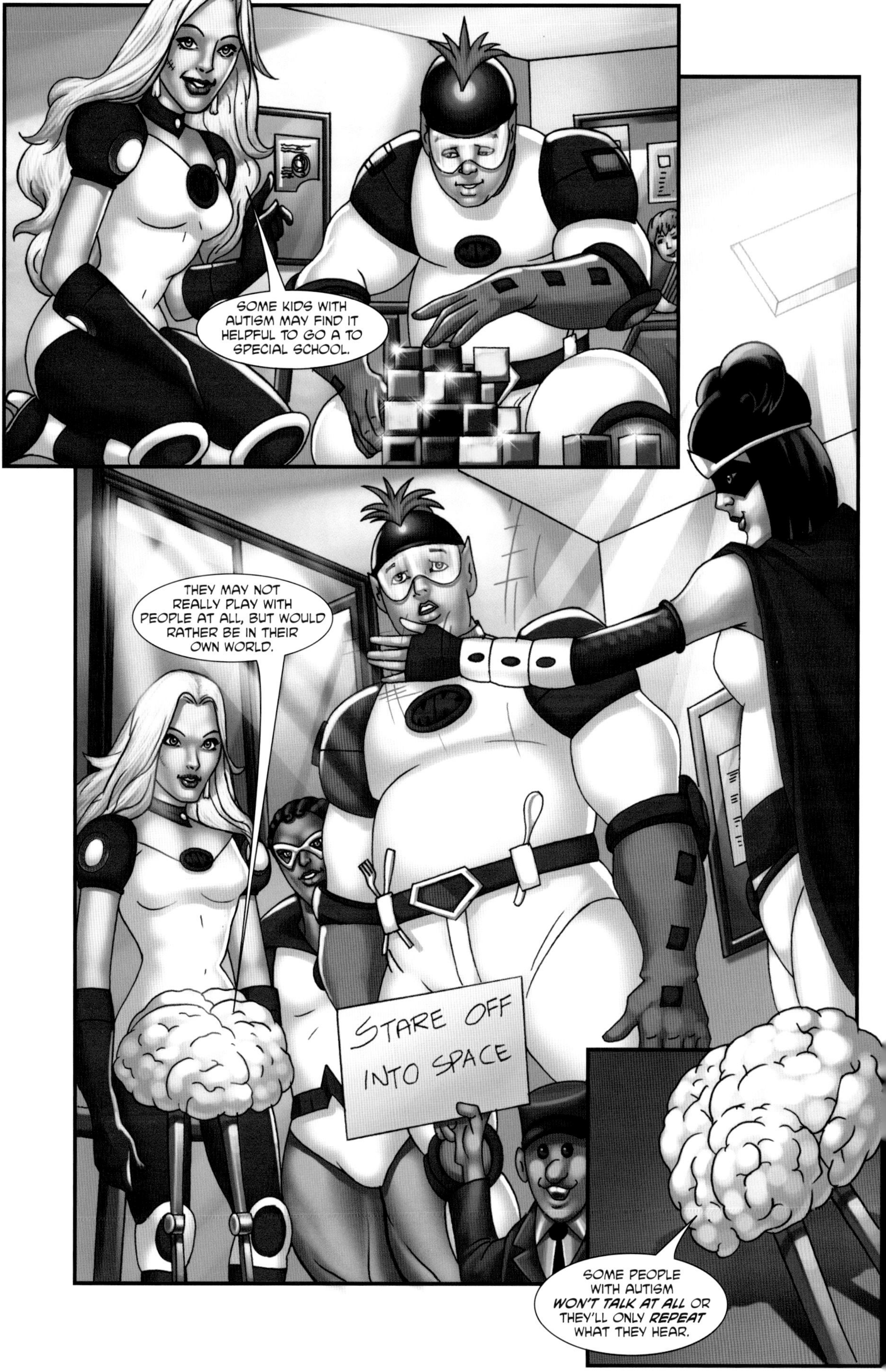
SOME KIDS WITH AUTISM MAY FIND IT HELPFUL TO GO A TO SPECIAL SCHOOL.
THEY MAY NOT REALLY PLAY WITH PEOPLE AT ALL, BUT WOULD RATHER BE IN THEIR OWN WORLD.
STARE OFF INTO SPACE
SOME PEOPLE WITH AUTISM *WON'T TALK AT ALL* OR THEY'LL ONLY *REPEAT* WHAT THEY HEAR.

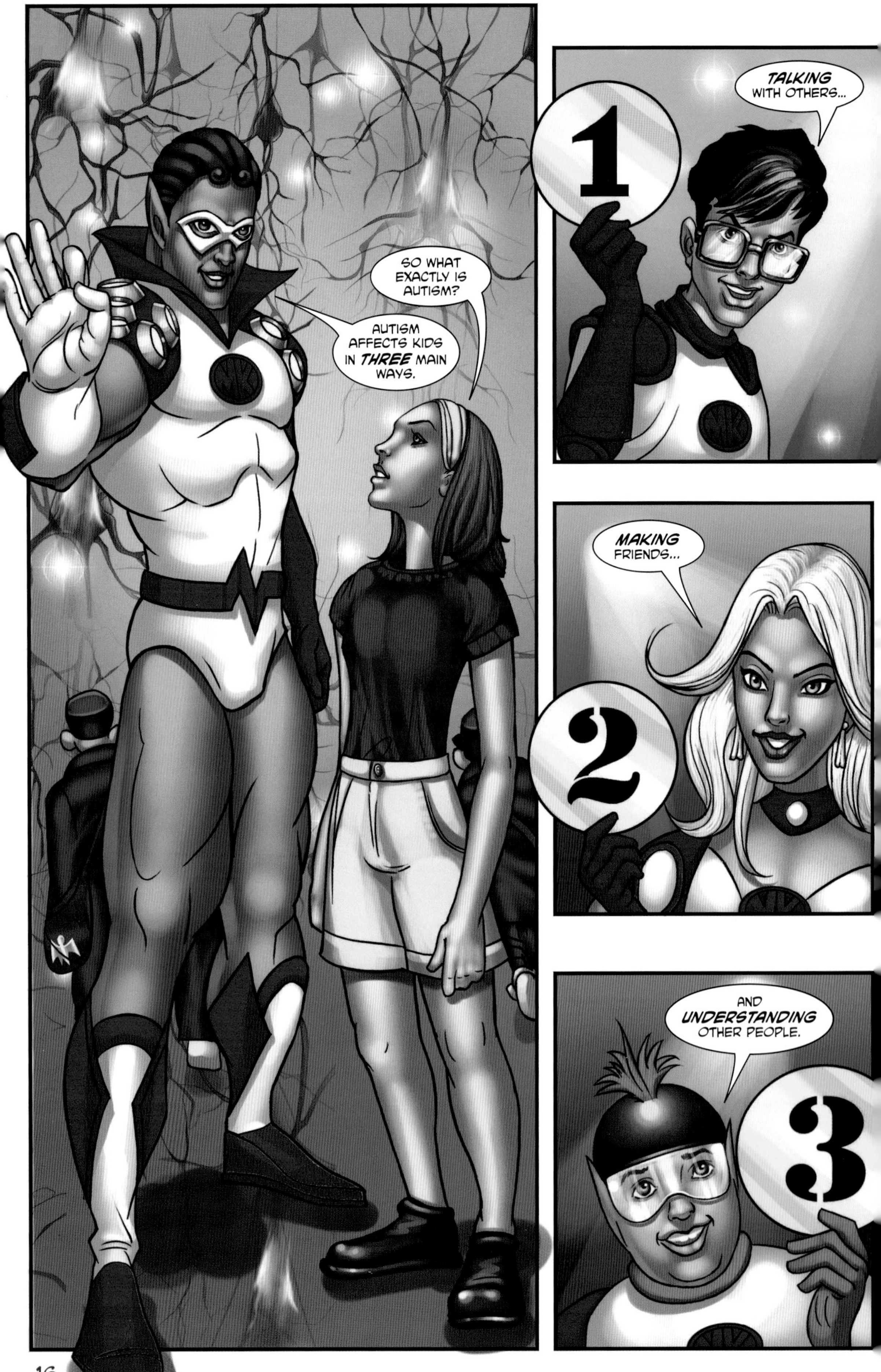
SO WHAT EXACTLY IS AUTISM?
AUTISM AFFECTS KIDS IN THREE MAIN WAYS.
1
TALKING WITH OTHERS...
MAKING FRIENDS...
2
AND UNDERSTANDING OTHER PEOPLE.
3

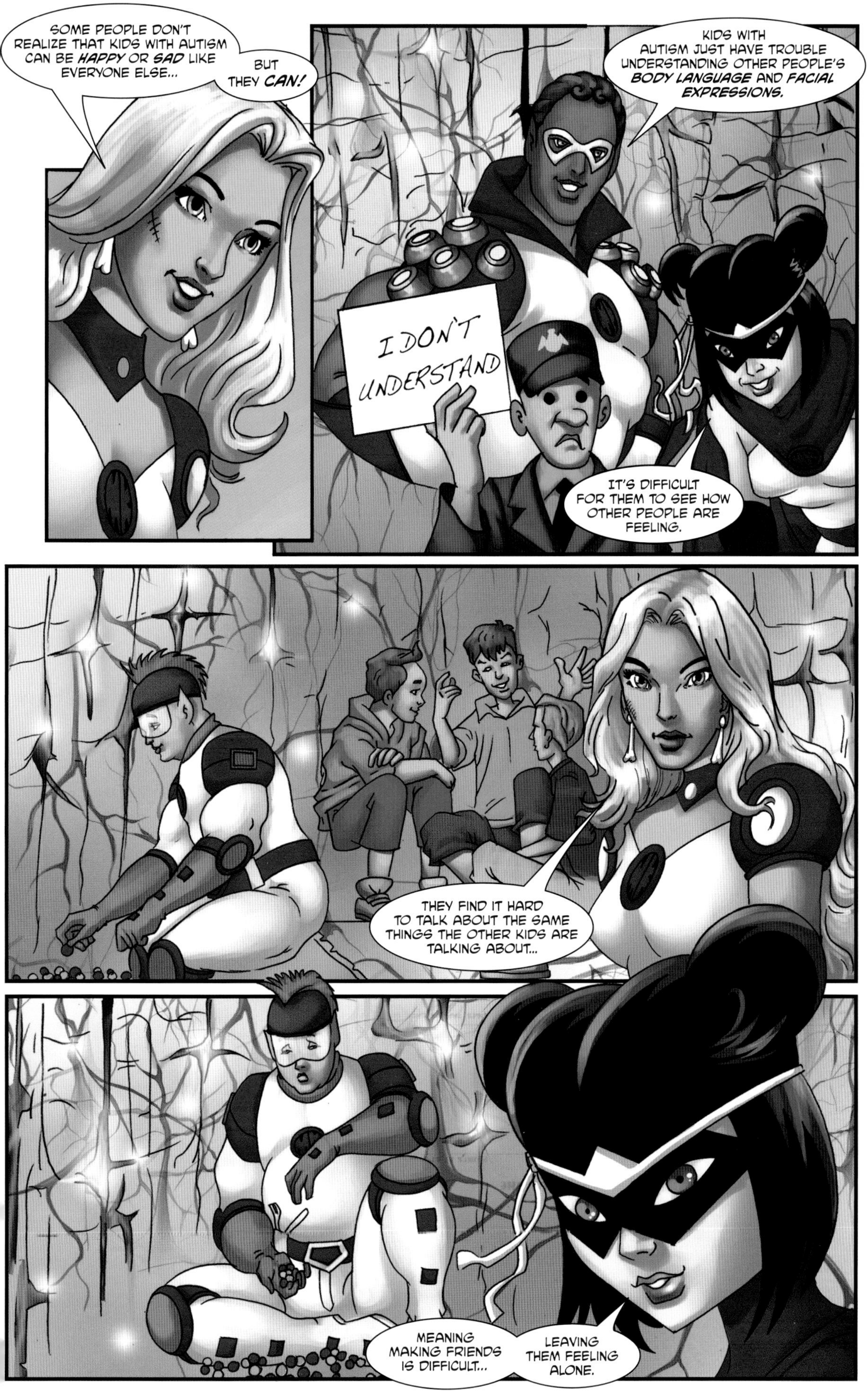
SOME PEOPLE DON'T REALIZE THAT KIDS WITH AUTISM CAN BE HAPPY OR SAD LIKE EVERYONE ELSE...
BUT THEY CAN!
KIDS WITH AUTISM JUST HAVE TROUBLE UNDERSTANDING OTHER PEOPLE'S BODY LANGUAGE AND FACIAL EXPRESSIONS.
I DON'T UNDERSTAND
IT'S DIFFICULT FOR THEM TO SEE HOW OTHER PEOPLE ARE FEELING.
THEY FIND IT HARD TO TALK ABOUT THE SAME THINGS THE OTHER KIDS ARE TALKING ABOUT...
MEANING MAKING FRIENDS IS DIFFICULT...
LEAVING THEM FEELING ALONE.

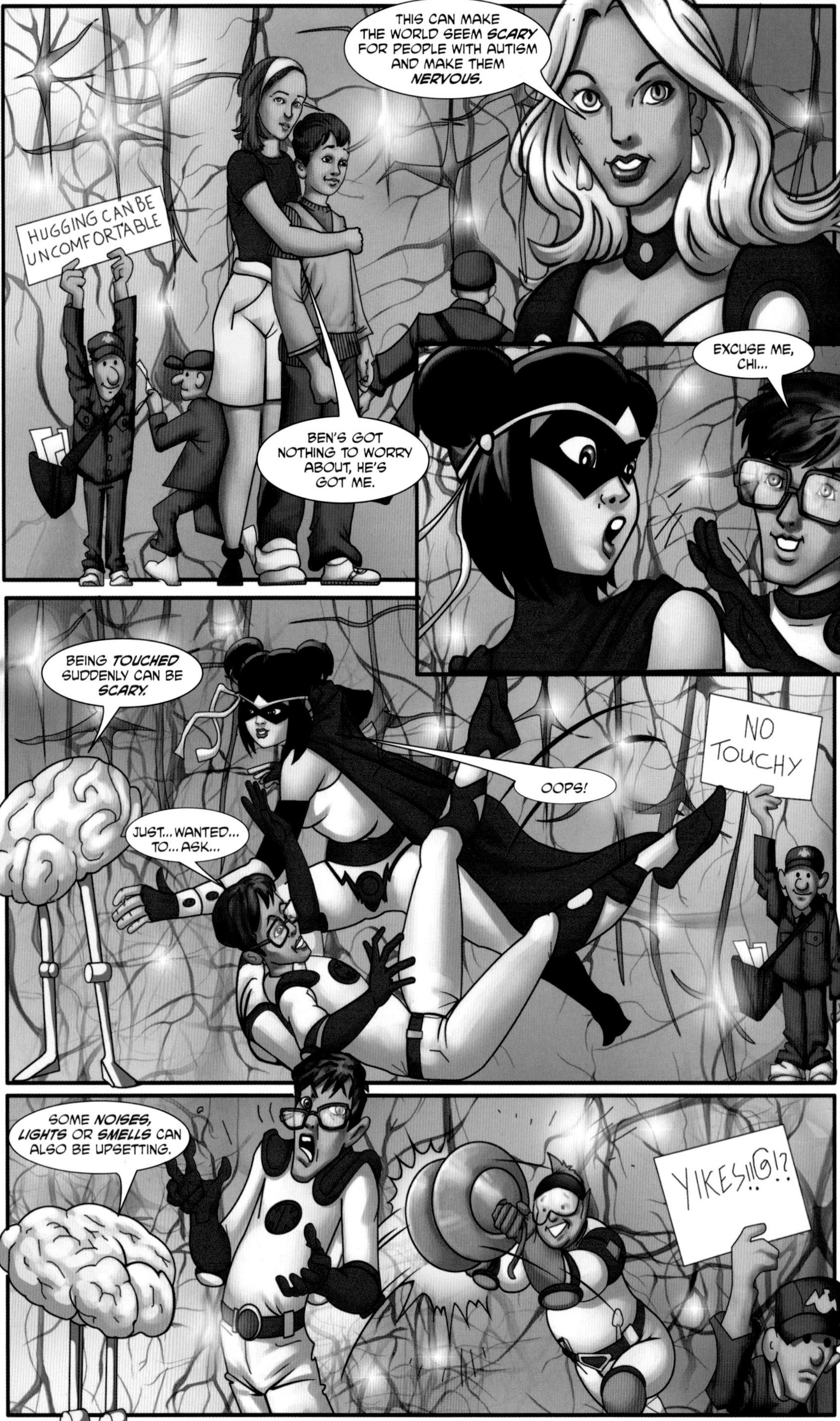
THIS CAN MAKE THE WORLD SEEM SCARY FOR PEOPLE WITH AUTISM AND MAKE THEM NERVOUS.
HUGGING CAN BE UNCOMFORTABLE
BEN'S GOT NOTHING TO WORRY ABOUT, HE'S GOT ME.
EXCUSE ME, CHI...
BEING TOUCHED SUDDENLY CAN BE SCARY.
OOPS!
NO TOUCHY
JUST... WANTED... TO... ASK...
SOME NOISES, LIGHTS OR SMELLS CAN ALSO BE UPSETTING.
YIKES!!@!?

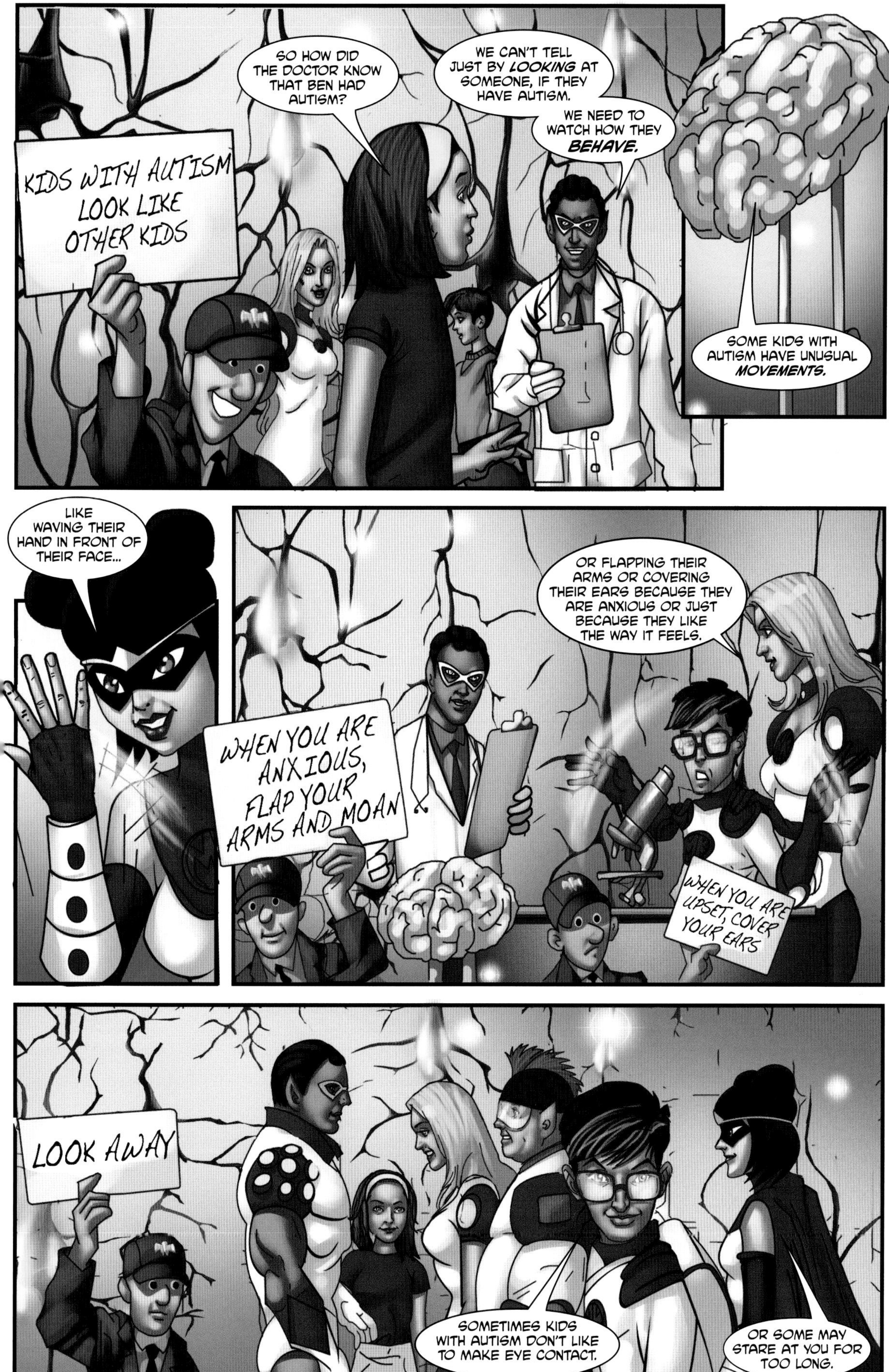
KIDS WITH AUTISM LOOK LIKE OTHER KIDS
SO HOW DID THE DOCTOR KNOW THAT BEN HAD AUTISM?
WE CAN'T TELL JUST BY *LOOKING* AT SOMEONE, IF THEY HAVE AUTISM.
WE NEED TO WATCH HOW THEY **BEHAVE.**
SOME KIDS WITH AUTISM HAVE UNUSUAL ***MOVEMENTS.***
LIKE WAVING THEIR HAND IN FRONT OF THEIR FACE...
OR FLAPPING THEIR ARMS OR COVERING THEIR EARS BECAUSE THEY ARE ANXIOUS OR JUST BECAUSE THEY LIKE THE WAY IT FEELS.
WHEN YOU ARE ANXIOUS, FLAP YOUR ARMS AND MOAN
WHEN YOU ARE UPSET, COVER YOUR EARS
LOOK AWAY
SOMETIMES KIDS WITH AUTISM DON'T LIKE TO MAKE EYE CONTACT.
OR SOME MAY STARE AT YOU FOR TOO LONG.

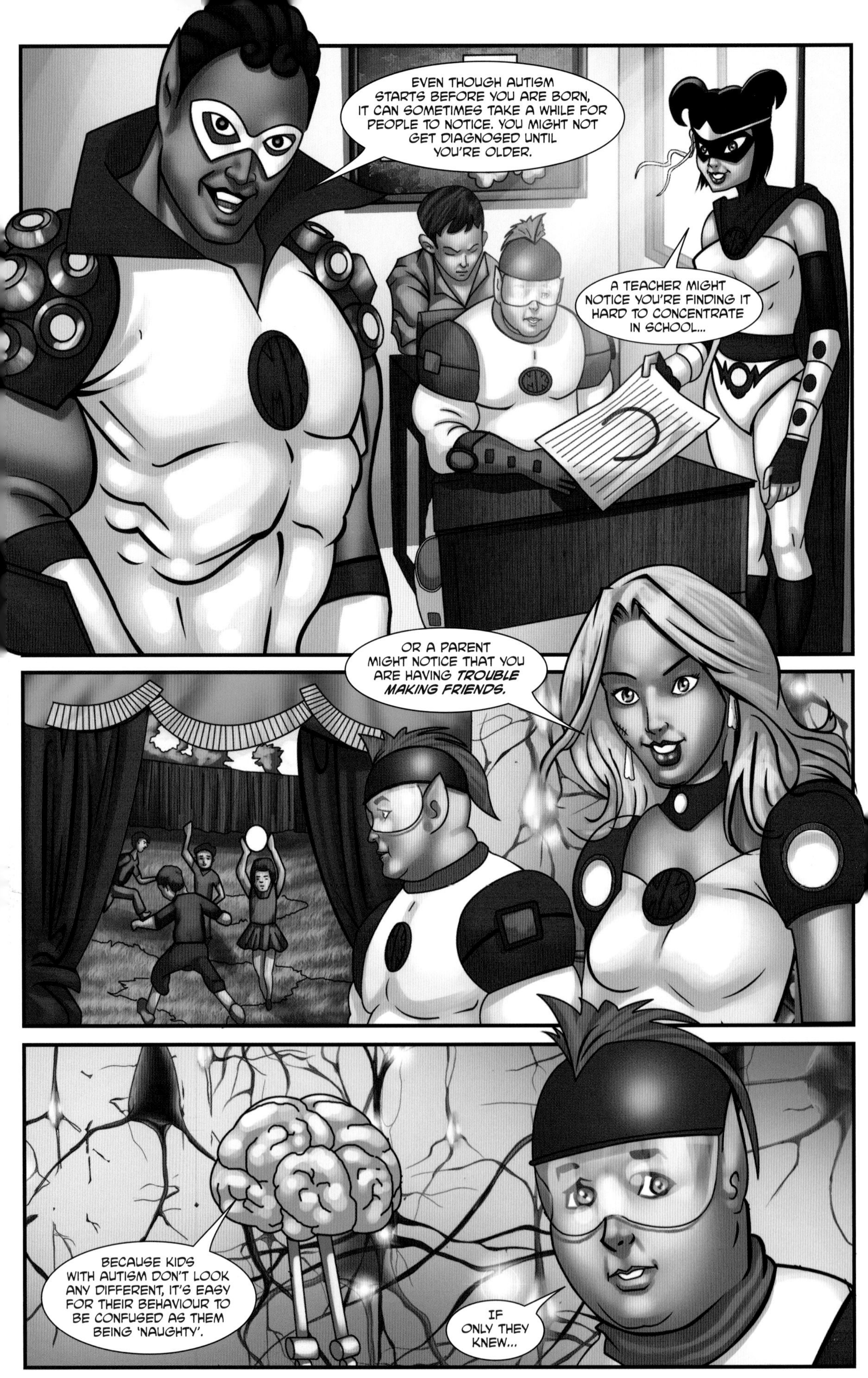
EVEN THOUGH AUTISM STARTS BEFORE YOU ARE BORN, IT CAN SOMETIMES TAKE A WHILE FOR PEOPLE TO NOTICE. YOU MIGHT NOT GET DIAGNOSED UNTIL YOU'RE OLDER.
A TEACHER MIGHT NOTICE YOU'RE FINDING IT HARD TO CONCENTRATE IN SCHOOL...
OR A PARENT MIGHT NOTICE THAT YOU ARE HAVING *TROUBLE MAKING FRIENDS.*
BECAUSE KIDS WITH AUTISM DON'T LOOK ANY DIFFERENT, IT'S EASY FOR THEIR BEHAVIOUR TO BE CONFUSED AS THEM BEING 'NAUGHTY'.
IF ONLY THEY KNEW...

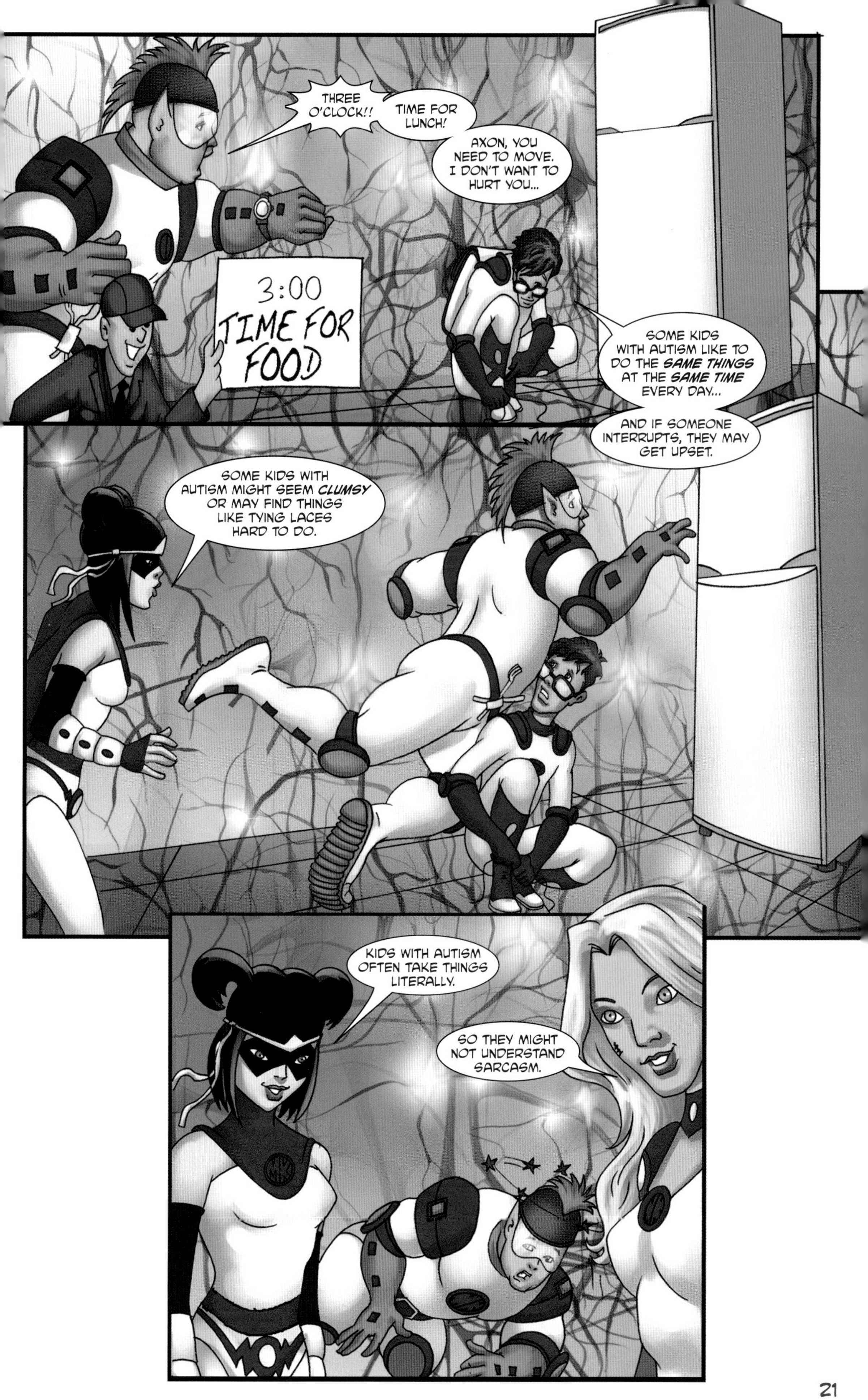
THREE O'CLOCK!!
TIME FOR LUNCH!
AXON, YOU NEED TO MOVE. I DON'T WANT TO HURT YOU...
3:00 TIME FOR FOOD
SOME KIDS WITH AUTISM LIKE TO DO THE SAME THINGS AT THE SAME TIME EVERY DAY...
AND IF SOMEONE INTERRUPTS, THEY MAY GET UPSET.
SOME KIDS WITH AUTISM MIGHT SEEM CLUMSY OR MAY FIND THINGS LIKE TYING LACES HARD TO DO.
KIDS WITH AUTISM OFTEN TAKE THINGS LITERALLY.
SO THEY MIGHT NOT UNDERSTAND SARCASM.

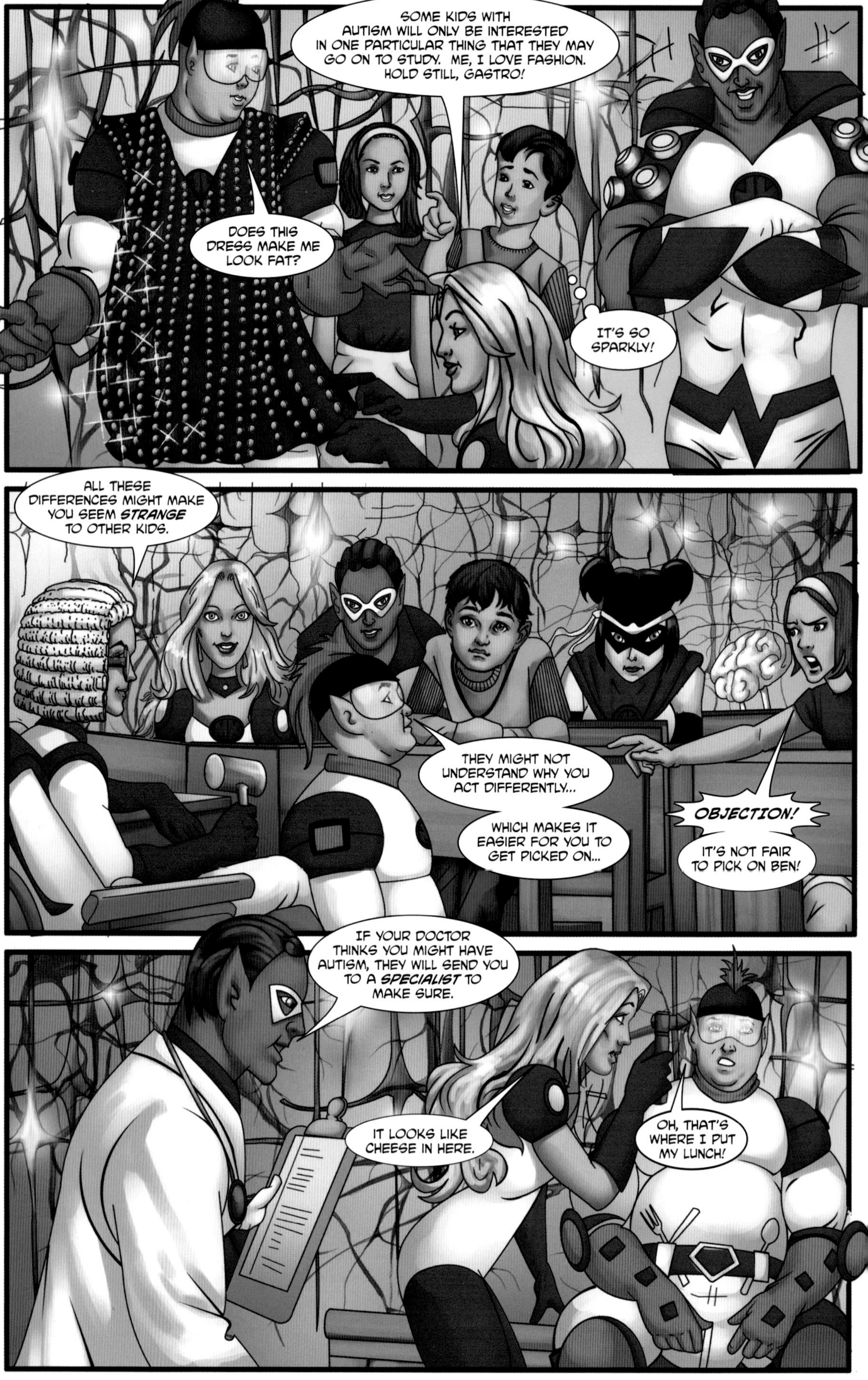
SOME KIDS WITH AUTISM WILL ONLY BE INTERESTED IN ONE PARTICULAR THING THAT THEY MAY GO ON TO STUDY. ME, I LOVE FASHION. HOLD STILL, GASTRO!
DOES THIS DRESS MAKE ME LOOK FAT?
IT'S SO SPARKLY!
ALL THESE DIFFERENCES MIGHT MAKE YOU SEEM *STRANGE* TO OTHER KIDS.
THEY MIGHT NOT UNDERSTAND WHY YOU ACT DIFFERENTLY...
WHICH MAKES IT EASIER FOR YOU TO GET PICKED ON...
OBJECTION!
IT'S NOT FAIR TO PICK ON BEN!
IF YOUR DOCTOR THINKS YOU MIGHT HAVE AUTISM, THEY WILL SEND YOU TO A *SPECIALIST* TO MAKE SURE.
IT LOOKS LIKE CHEESE IN HERE.
OH, THAT'S WHERE I PUT MY LUNCH!

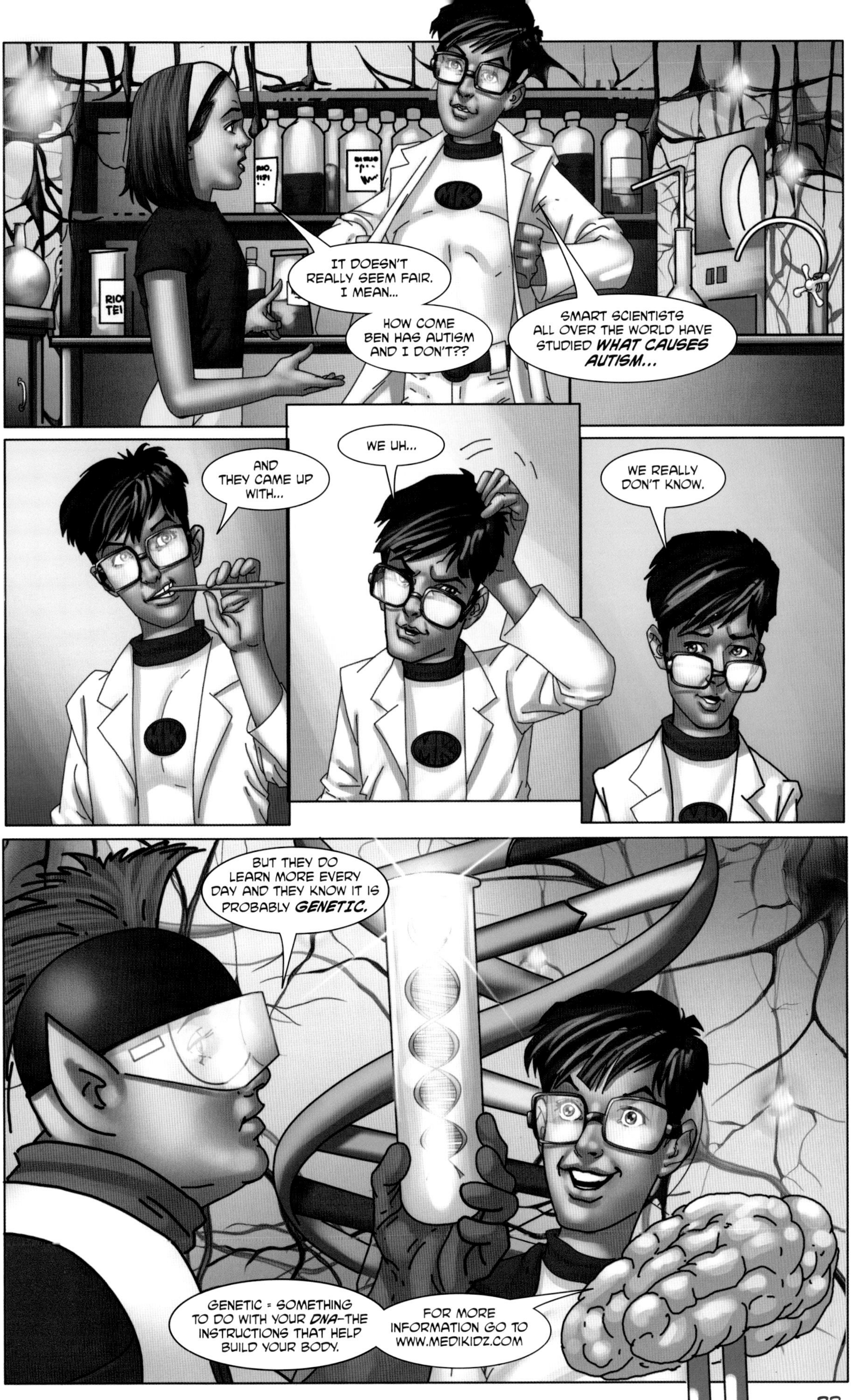

IT DOESN'T REALLY SEEM FAIR. I MEAN...
HOW COME BEN HAS AUTISM AND I DON'T??
SMART SCIENTISTS ALL OVER THE WORLD HAVE STUDIED ***WHAT CAUSES AUTISM...***
AND THEY CAME UP WITH...
WE UH...
WE REALLY DON'T KNOW.
BUT THEY DO LEARN MORE EVERY DAY AND THEY KNOW IT IS PROBABLY ***GENETIC.***
GENETIC = SOMETHING TO DO WITH YOUR *DNA*–THE INSTRUCTIONS THAT HELP BUILD YOUR BODY.
FOR MORE INFORMATION GO TO WWW.MEDIKIDZ.COM

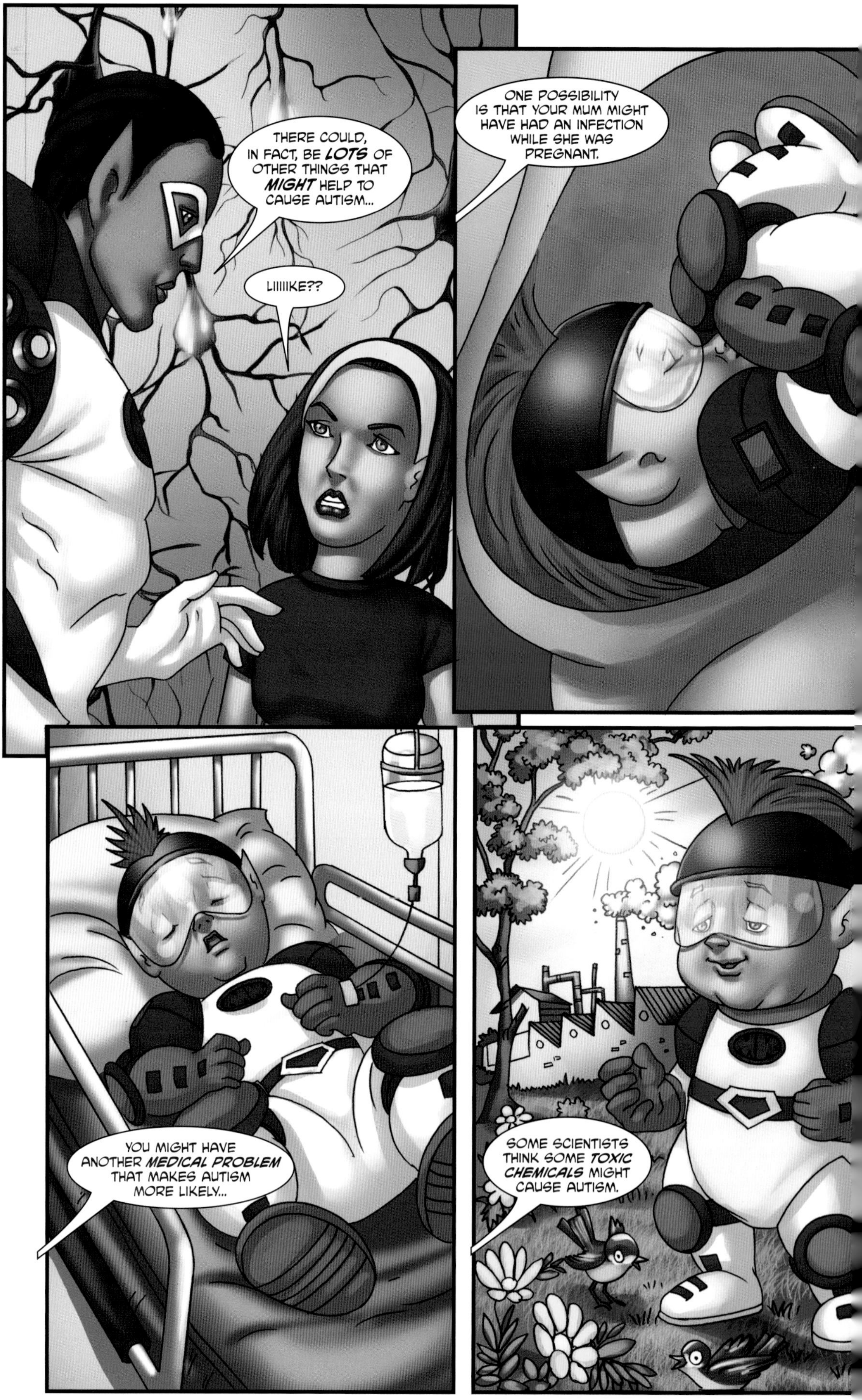
THERE COULD, IN FACT, BE LOTS OF OTHER THINGS THAT MIGHT HELP TO CAUSE AUTISM...
LIIIIKE??
ONE POSSIBILITY IS THAT YOUR MUM MIGHT HAVE HAD AN INFECTION WHILE SHE WAS PREGNANT.
YOU MIGHT HAVE ANOTHER MEDICAL PROBLEM THAT MAKES AUTISM MORE LIKELY...
SOME SCIENTISTS THINK SOME TOXIC CHEMICALS MIGHT CAUSE AUTISM.

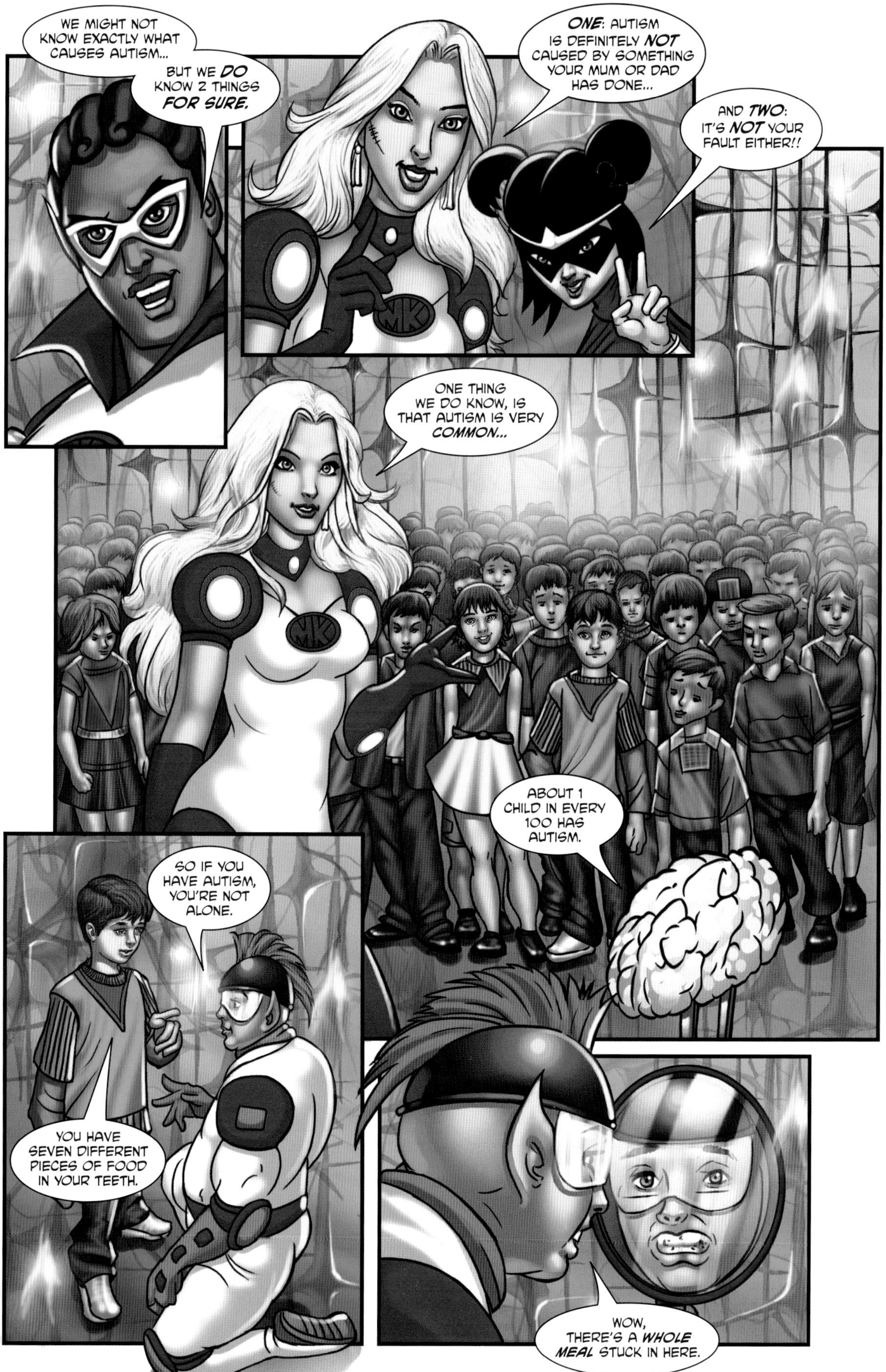
WE MIGHT NOT KNOW EXACTLY WHAT CAUSES AUTISM...
BUT WE **DO** KNOW 2 THINGS **FOR SURE.**
ONE: AUTISM IS DEFINITELY **NOT** CAUSED BY SOMETHING YOUR MUM OR DAD HAS DONE...
AND **TWO**: IT'S **NOT** YOUR FAULT EITHER!!
ONE THING WE DO KNOW, IS THAT AUTISM IS VERY *COMMON...*
ABOUT 1 CHILD IN EVERY 100 HAS AUTISM.
SO IF YOU HAVE AUTISM, YOU'RE NOT ALONE.
YOU HAVE SEVEN DIFFERENT PIECES OF FOOD IN YOUR TEETH.
WOW, THERE'S A **WHOLE MEAL** STUCK IN HERE.

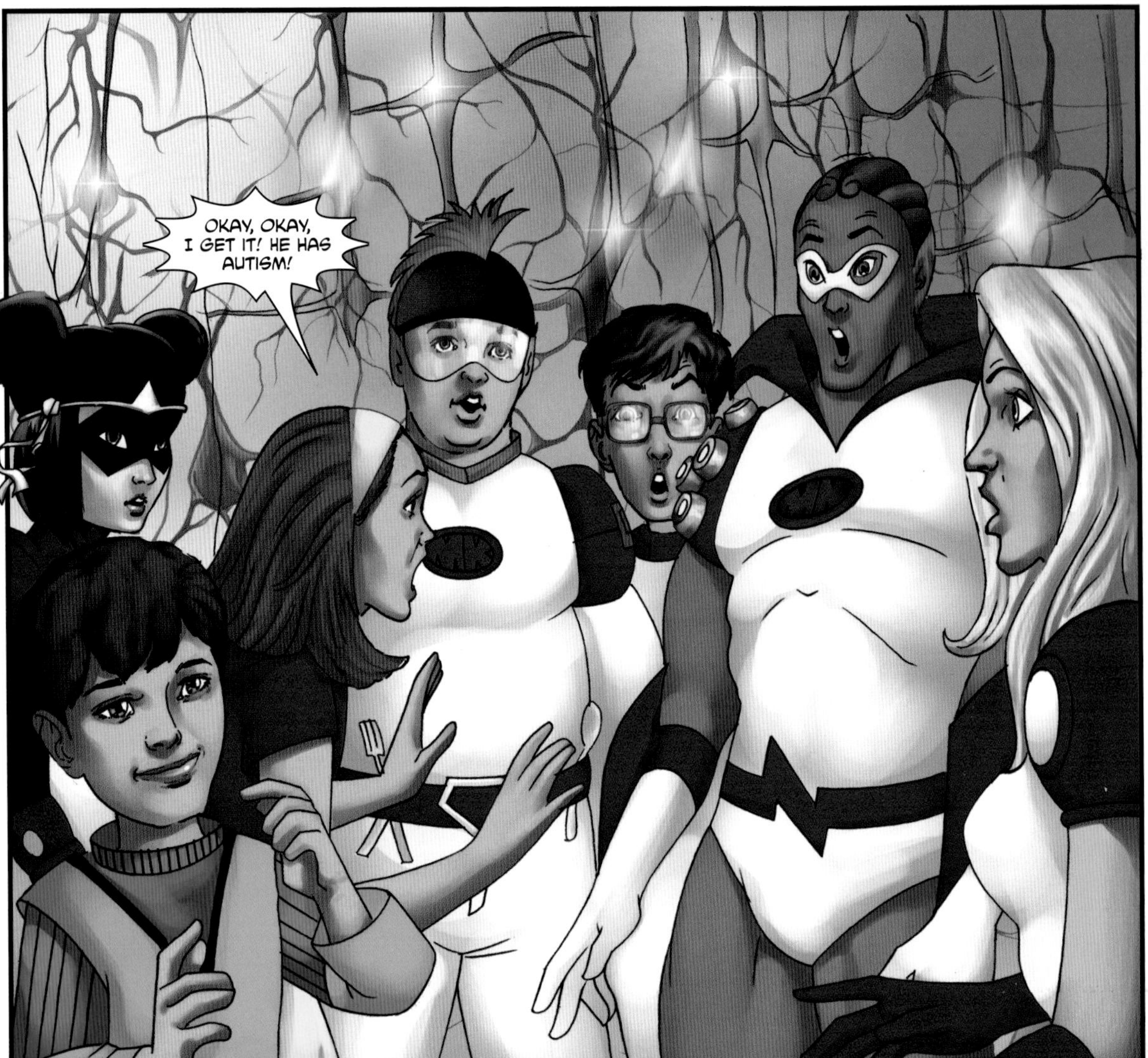
OKAY, OKAY, I GET IT! HE HAS AUTISM!

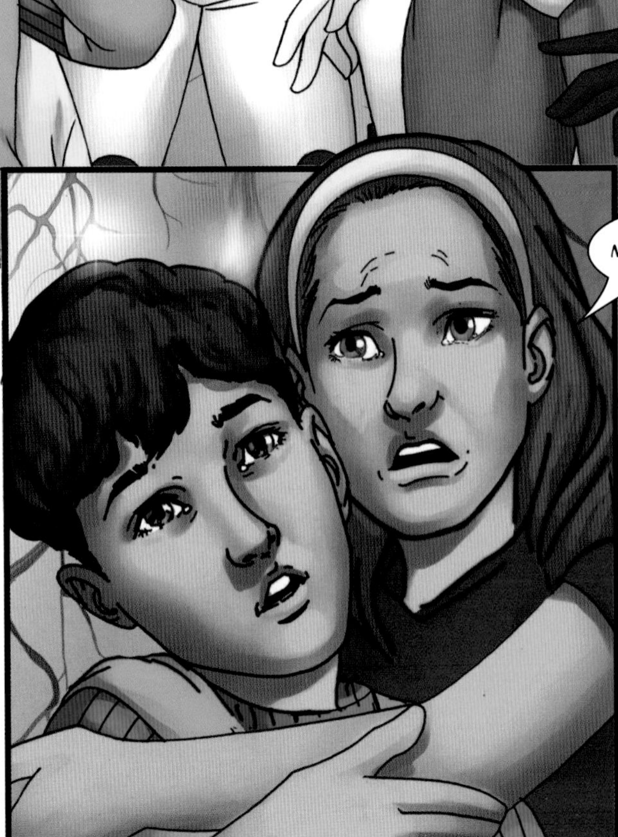
JUST TELL ME HOW TO MAKE HIM BETTER.

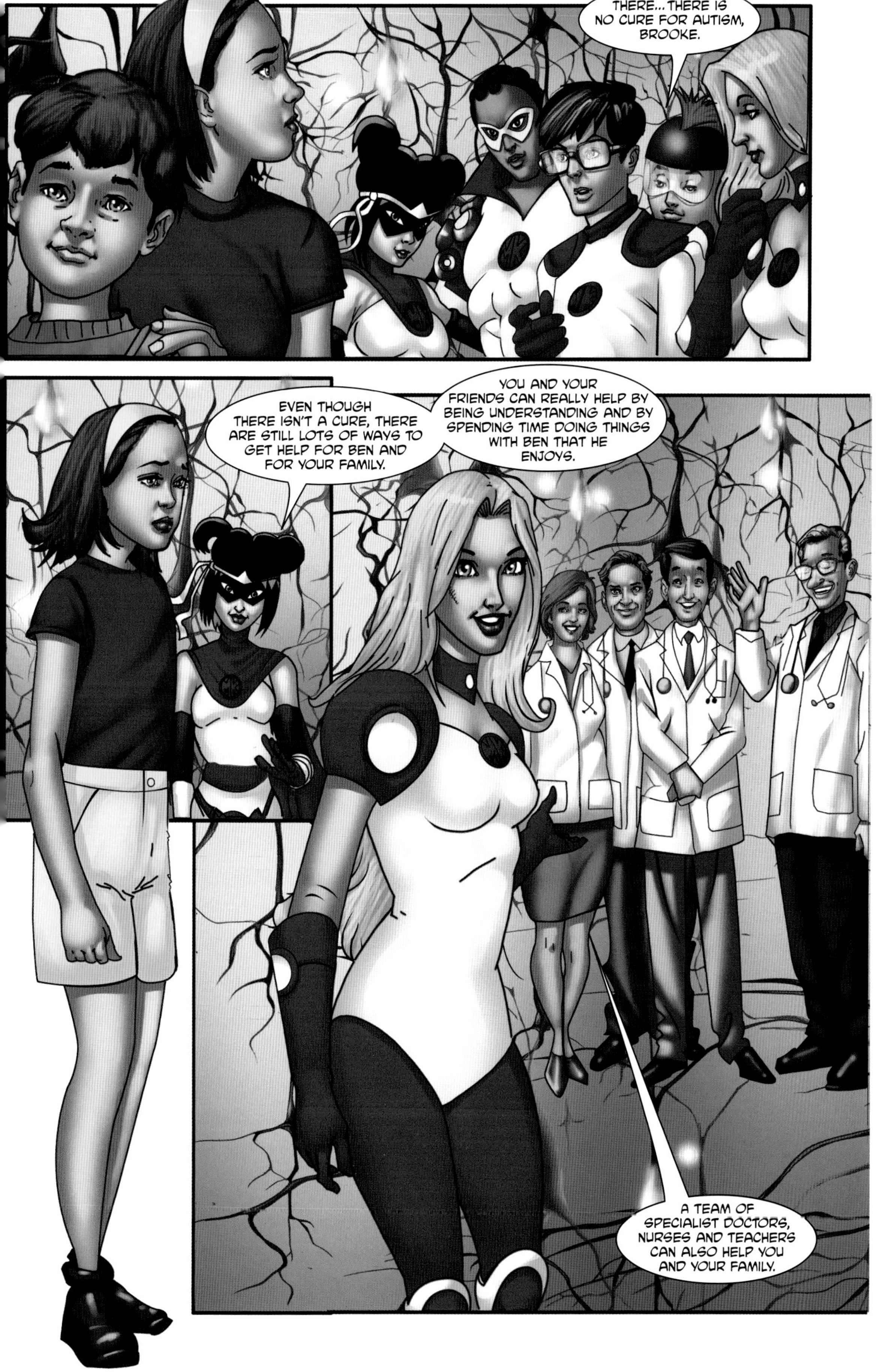
THERE... THERE IS NO CURE FOR AUTISM, BROOKE.
EVEN THOUGH THERE ISN'T A CURE, THERE ARE STILL LOTS OF WAYS TO GET HELP FOR BEN AND FOR YOUR FAMILY.
YOU AND YOUR FRIENDS CAN REALLY HELP BY BEING UNDERSTANDING AND BY SPENDING TIME DOING THINGS WITH BEN THAT HE ENJOYS.
A TEAM OF SPECIALIST DOCTORS, NURSES AND TEACHERS CAN ALSO HELP YOU AND YOUR FAMILY.

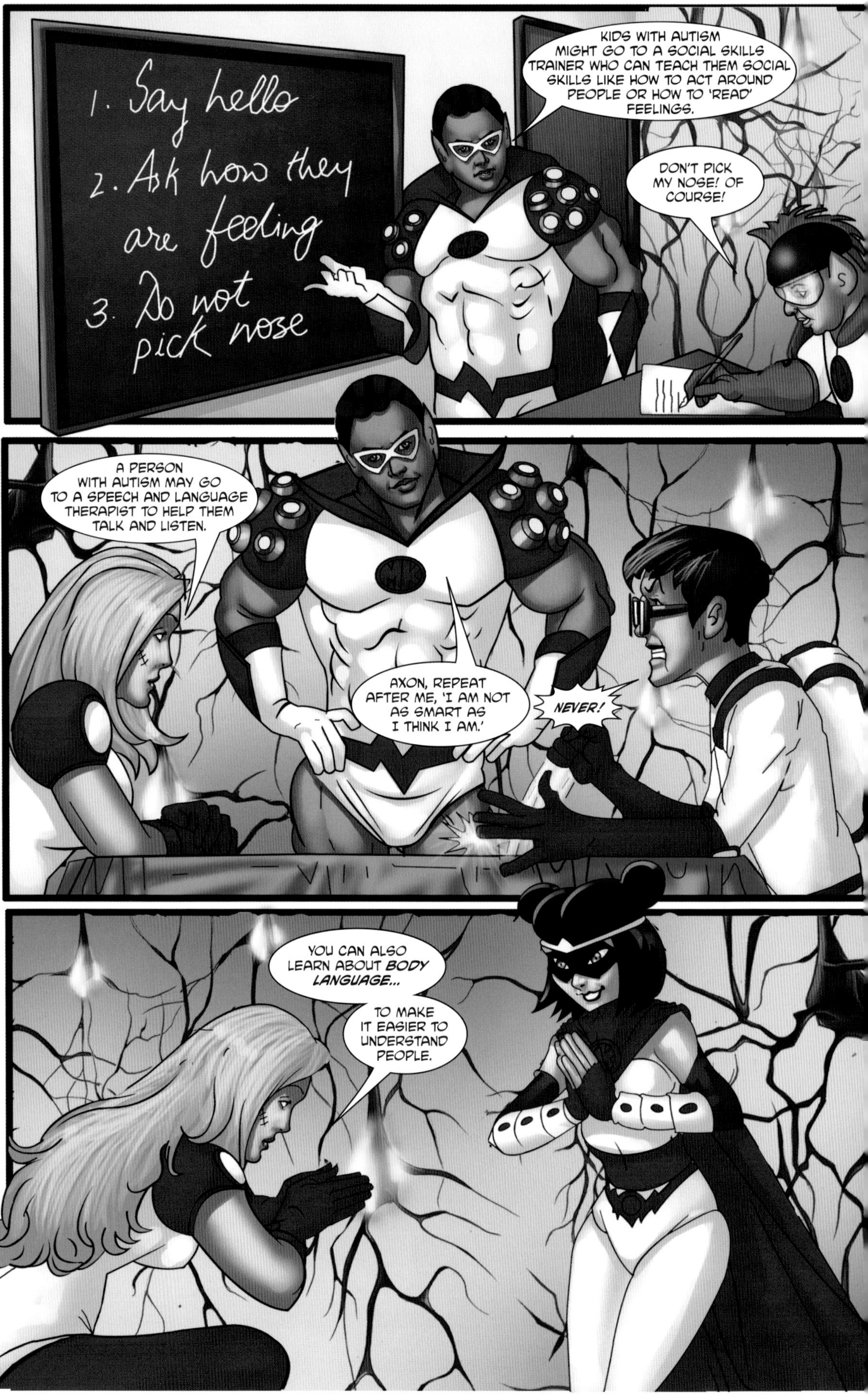
1. Say hello
2. Ask how they are feeling
3. Do not pick nose
KIDS WITH AUTISM MIGHT GO TO A SOCIAL SKILLS TRAINER WHO CAN TEACH THEM SOCIAL SKILLS LIKE HOW TO ACT AROUND PEOPLE OR HOW TO 'READ' FEELINGS.
DON'T PICK MY NOSE! OF COURSE!
A PERSON WITH AUTISM MAY GO TO A SPEECH AND LANGUAGE THERAPIST TO HELP THEM TALK AND LISTEN.
AXON, REPEAT AFTER ME, 'I AM NOT AS SMART AS I THINK I AM.'
NEVER!
YOU CAN ALSO LEARN ABOUT BODY LANGUAGE...
TO MAKE IT EASIER TO UNDERSTAND PEOPLE.

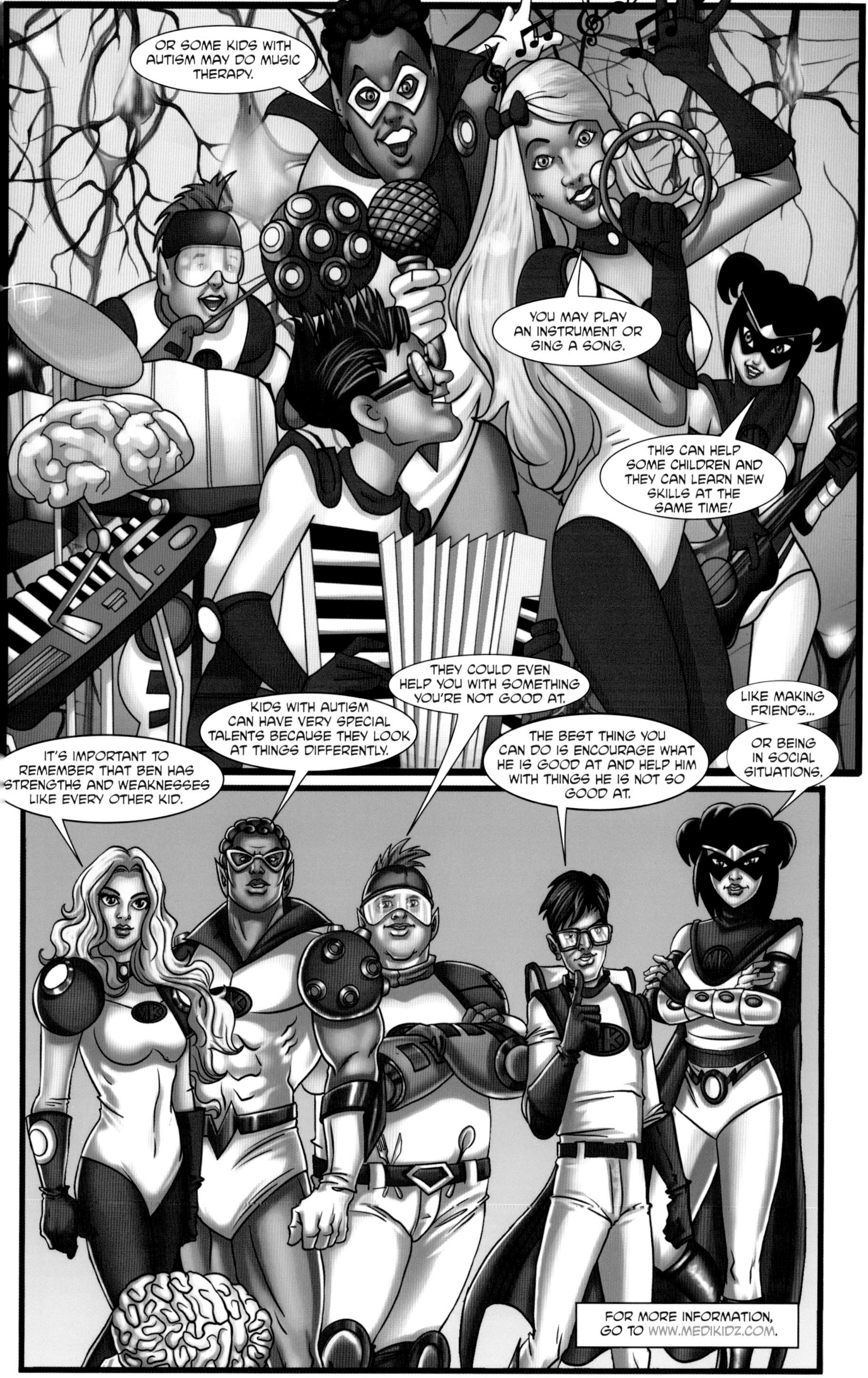

OR SOME KIDS WITH AUTISM MAY DO MUSIC THERAPY.
YOU MAY PLAY AN INSTRUMENT OR SING A SONG.
THIS CAN HELP SOME CHILDREN AND THEY CAN LEARN NEW SKILLS AT THE SAME TIME!
IT'S IMPORTANT TO REMEMBER THAT BEN HAS STRENGTHS AND WEAKNESSES LIKE EVERY OTHER KID.
KIDS WITH AUTISM CAN HAVE VERY SPECIAL TALENTS BECAUSE THEY LOOK AT THINGS DIFFERENTLY.
THEY COULD EVEN HELP YOU WITH SOMETHING YOU'RE NOT GOOD AT.
THE BEST THING YOU CAN DO IS ENCOURAGE WHAT HE IS GOOD AT AND HELP HIM WITH THINGS HE IS NOT SO GOOD AT.
LIKE MAKING FRIENDS...
OR BEING IN SOCIAL SITUATIONS.
FOR MORE INFORMATION, GO TO WWW.MEDIKIDZ.COM.

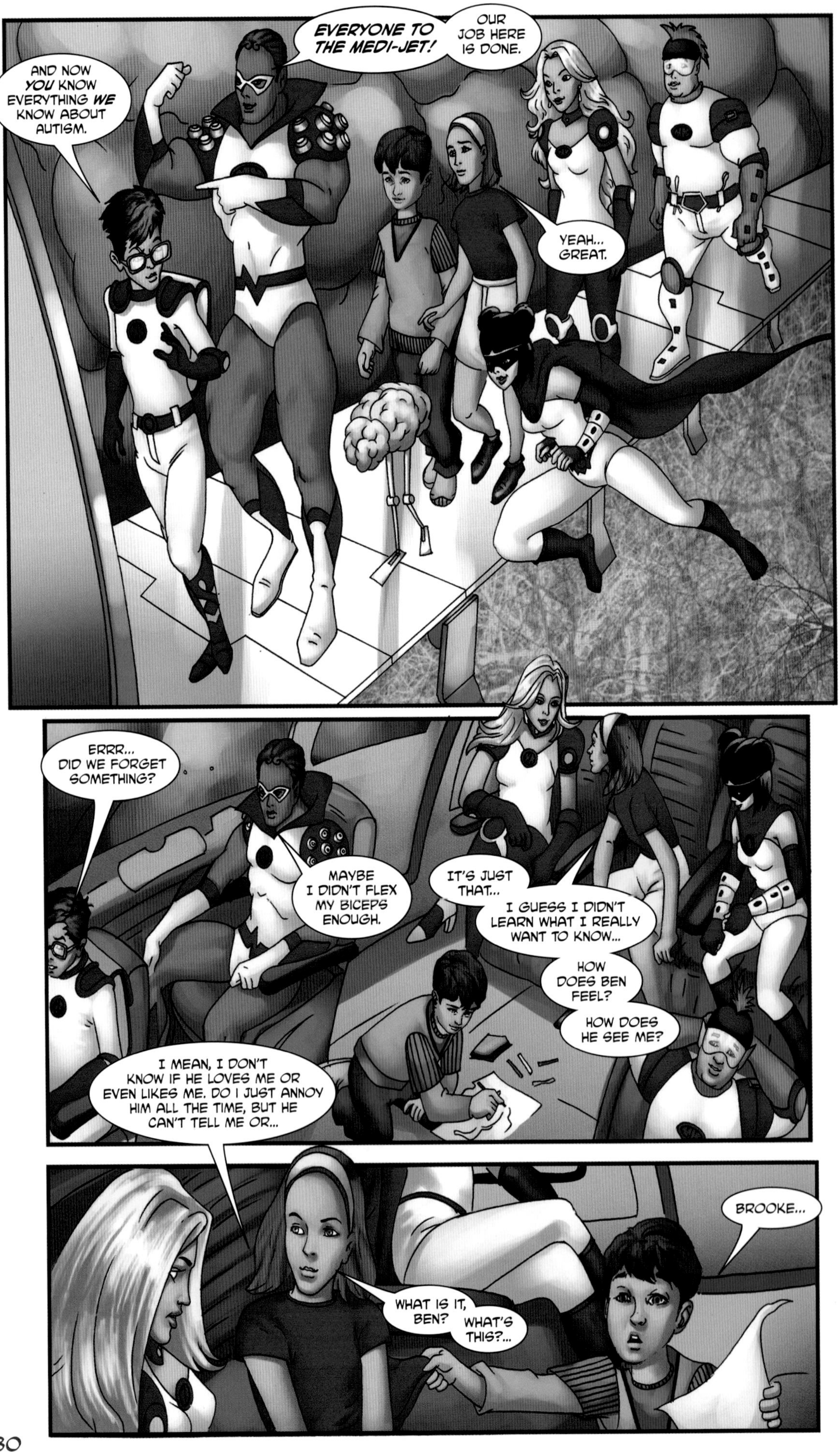
AND NOW *YOU* KNOW EVERYTHING *WE* KNOW ABOUT AUTISM.
EVERYONE TO THE MEDI-JET!
OUR JOB HERE IS DONE.
YEAH... GREAT.
ERRR... DID WE FORGET SOMETHING?
MAYBE I DIDN'T FLEX MY BICEPS ENOUGH.
IT'S JUST THAT...
I GUESS I DIDN'T LEARN WHAT I REALLY WANT TO KNOW...
HOW DOES BEN FEEL?
HOW DOES HE SEE ME?
I MEAN, I DON'T KNOW IF HE LOVES ME OR EVEN LIKES ME. DO I JUST ANNOY HIM ALL THE TIME, BUT HE CAN'T TELL ME OR...
BROOKE...
WHAT IS IT, BEN?
WHAT'S THIS?...

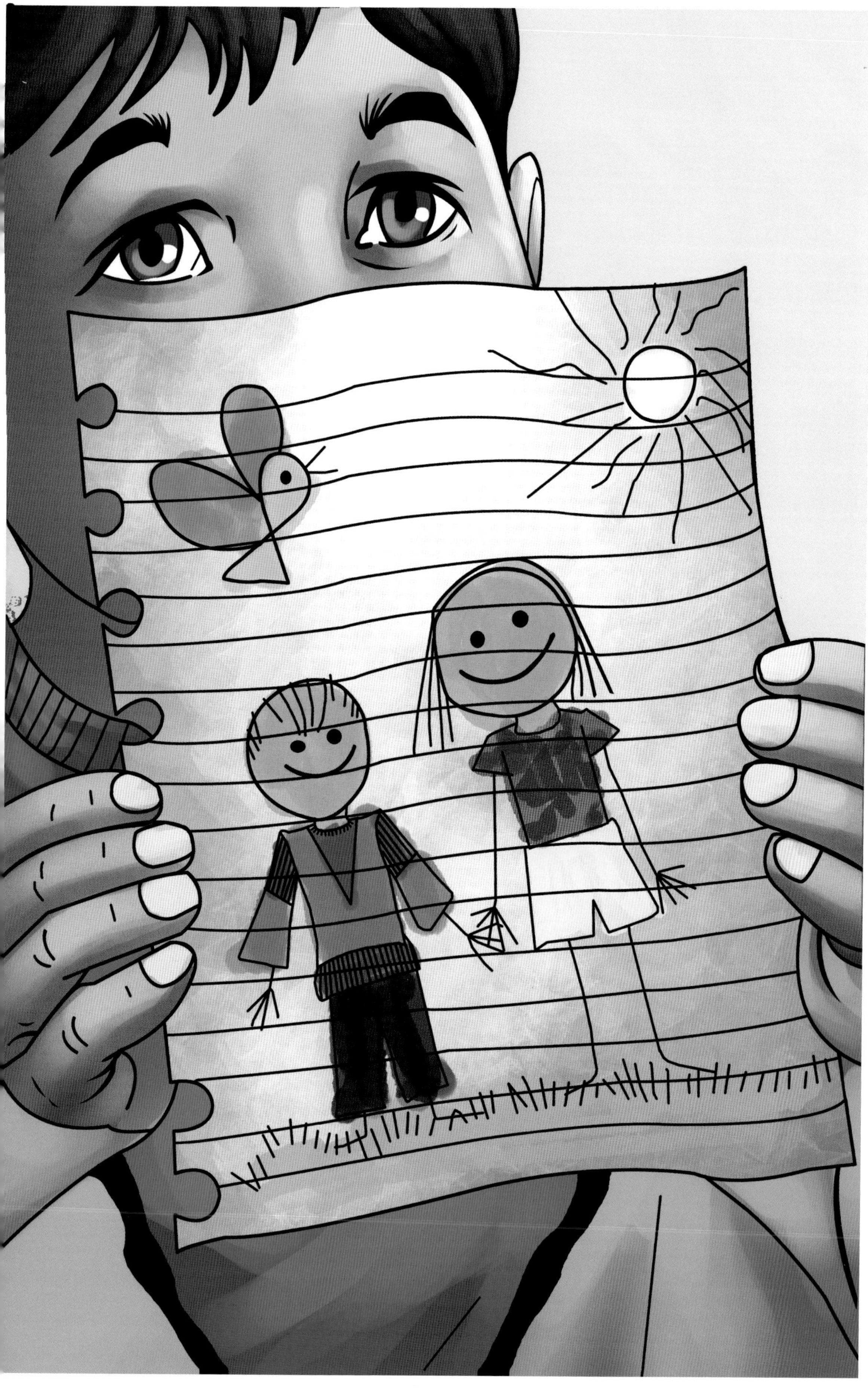

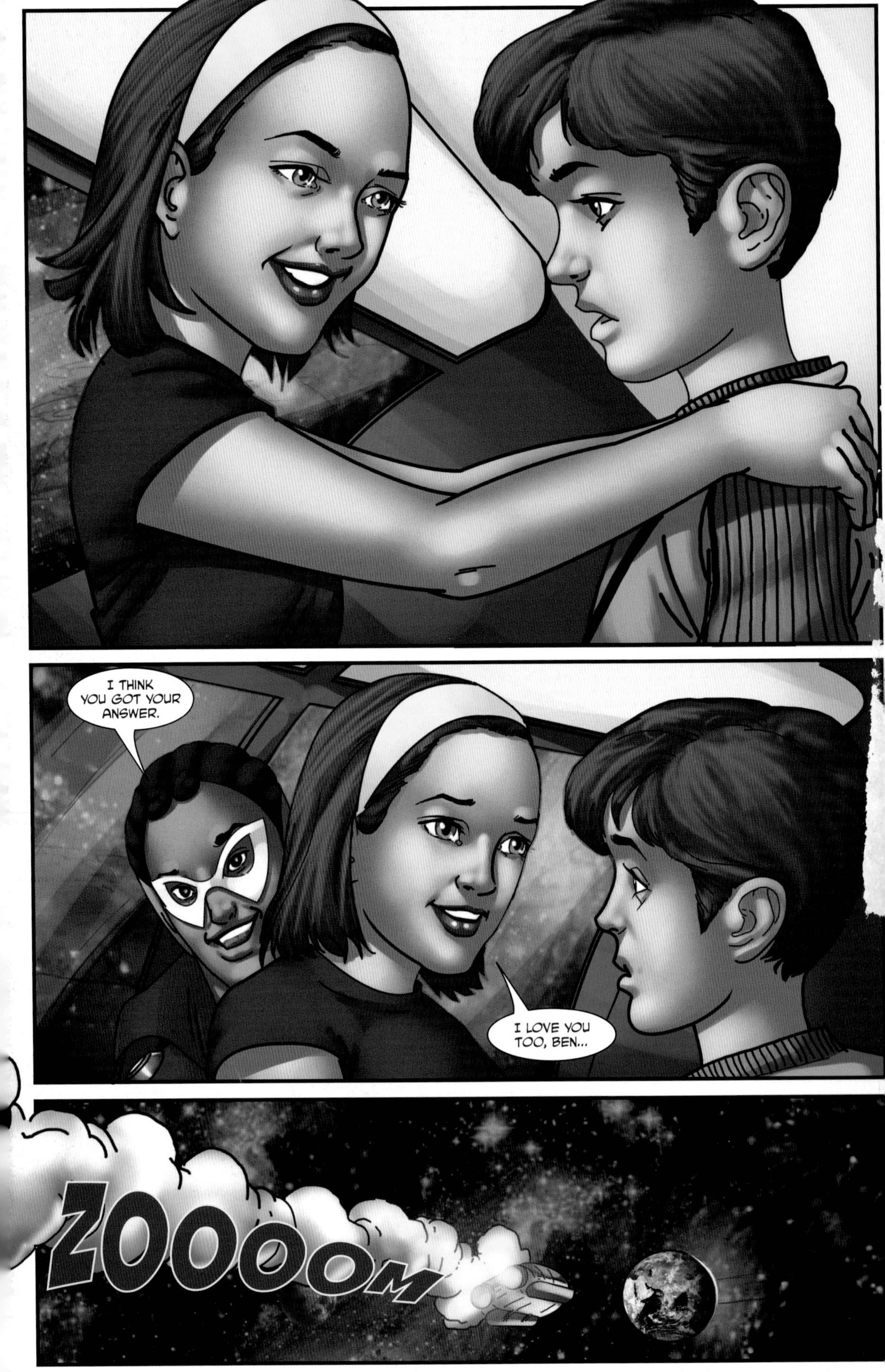
I THINK YOU GOT YOUR ANSWER.
I LOVE YOU TOO, BEN...
ZOOOOM